The Beginner's Guide to Machine Sewing

First published in 2026

Search Press Limited
Wellwood, North Farm Road,
Tunbridge Wells, Kent TN2 3DR

Photographs on pages 1, 7, 9, 11, 12–13, 18–19, 32–33, 37, 39, 43, 45, 51, 53 (BR), 55, 58, 53, 64, 71 (T), 73, 74, 77 (BR), 85, 86, 95, 96, 101 (R), 107, 108, 113 (BR), 115, 116, 117 and 118 by Stacy Grant (www.stacygrant.co.uk)

Photographs on pages 10, 16–17, 27 (M+B), 56 (BL), 78 and 91 (TR) by Mark Davison (www.markdavison.com)

All other photographs by Debbie von Grabler-Crozier

ISBN: 978-1-80092-379-9
ebook ISBN: 978-1-80093-358-3

Bookmarked Hub
Extra copies of the templates are available to download free from the website Bookmarked Hub. Search for this book by title or ISBN: the files can be found under 'Book Extras'. Membership of the Bookmarked online community is free: www.bookmarkedhub.com

Publishers' notes
Metric measurements are used in this book; the imperial conversions are rounded to the nearest ⅛in. Always use either metric or imperial measurements, not a combination of both.

The Publishers and author can accept no responsibility for any consequences arising from the information, advice or instructions given in this publication.

For errata, please visit our website (www.searchpress.com) or the Bookmarked Hub (www.bookmarkedhub.com).

GPSR information can be found at www.searchpress.com

Printed in China, TT052026

Dedication

This book, just like everything that I do, is dedicated to my husband Rob and my son Tristan. Without you both, I am nothing at all.

Acknowledgements

As usual, writing the acknowledgements ties me up in knots in case I miss anyone out. I am such a tiny part of the writing process and I am always overwhelmed (in the nicest possible way) when I stop to think about how many dedicated and talented hands my book manuscript passes through on its way to the recognizable form you see now.

But let me have a go at saying the proper thank-yous by starting with my family. My husband Rob and my son Tristan, our cocker spaniel Daisy and our cat, Checkmate. These four are the cornerstones of my existence. (The cat, mind you, is as gentle as gelignite in a crisis, and can be counted upon to say the most devastating things at the wrong time. But he is 19 years old now and allowed to be a grumpy old man.) Rob, Tris and Daisy have supported me all the way.

At Search Press, I want to say a heartfelt thanks to Sam, Becky and Emily, and all of the clever hands who have pummelled, shaped and moulded this book into the one that you have raced off to buy. I am waiting for the English language to come up with some really good words so that I can use them to show my proper appreciation. Thank you all, so, so much.

Without my industry collaborators, the projects would not look so nice (or even exist in this form), so thank you to Art Gallery Fabrics in the US and Jon at Adlico Fabrics in Denmark for supporting me. Always. Vlieseline® in Germany has provided me with all of the interfacing that I use, and Janome Deutschland gives me the best sewing machine in the world. Clover MFG in Japan is last but by no means least. I use Clover tools for everything and they are constantly coming up with new and thoughtful additions to the kit.

x

DEBBIE VON GRABLER-CROZIER

The Beginner's Guide to Machine Sewing

Easy techniques and 8 fun projects

SEARCH PRESS

Contents

Introduction

I was fortunate enough to have an engaged and committed mother and grandmother who passed on to me all of their knowledge, and I sucked it up like a dry sponge. Among many skills I learned, from baking bread and tending chickens to knitting and canning, one of these was learning to sew.

Being able to sew not only meant that my family and I would have clothes, and could mend them, but we could make useful, unique items frugally too. If we needed curtains, I could sew them at a fraction of the price of bought ones. Need a matching tablecloth for Christmas or a birthday? Give me an hour. Torn jeans? No problem – as soon as I mend this large rip in the leg, there are years of wear left in them. Then, when the jeans finally do wear out, I can transform the untorn leg into a bag to hold gardening tools. And I can salvage the hardware too.

Learning to sew at a young age is still something I consider a big lottery win, as not everyone is so lucky to have a mother and grandmother who can teach them to stitch. If you've always wanted to give it a go, or even thought 'Why sew something when you can buy it?', here is where a book like this one comes in. I want to show you how easy it is to get started with sewing, how simple sewing can be, and inspire you to explore more complex sewing projects too. There's nothing more rewarding than walking into a shop, seeing ready-made pillows, bags and more and thinking 'I can make that.' And, even better, I hope you will pass on your sewing skills to others too.

This book starts with the basics; you'll then build on those skills until you are making things that you never thought possible. You don't need much to get going either. A small piece of fabric or two and some basic tools and you are away.

Have fun and happy sewing!

Debbie xx

Tools and materials

You don't need an awful lot to get started and make something useful (and amazing looking too). Here are some of the things I cannot do without, and I will address each item as we meet it in the following chapters. Always buy the best that you can and have a look around in sales online or in store.

BASIC SEWING TOOLS

1. FABRIC SCISSORS

I recommend investing in a large pair of scissors – 12.5cm (5in) blades – to start with. NEVER use these scissors to cut anything other than fabric, as this blunts the blades. Keep your scissors sharp so that the fabric doesn't drag when cutting out.

2. SEAM RIPPER

For accidental stitches or removing temporary stitch lines, you'll need a seam ripper (sometimes called a quick unpick). Use the pointy end to undo individual stitches; to quickly undo a large seam, place the seam vertically between the pointy end and the ball tip, then push the seam ripper away from you.

3. HAND-SEWING NEEDLES

We'll be mainly machine sewing in this book, but there will be times when you'll need to hand sew, mostly to finish off work. Packs of five or seven needles that are a regular length and have an average eye size will cover most jobs.

4. THIMBLE

Experienced or newbie, you'll need one of these whenever you're hand sewing!

5. PINS AND CLIPS

There are so many pins available on the market – in time you'll have your preferences! I like to use flower-head pins as their longer length makes pinning for quiltmaking a breeze. However, glass-head pins are often a favourite with sewists as they're heat-proof, meaning you can press your makes with the pins left in. Fabric clips are excellent for situations where the seams are bulky, which you'll find in bagmaking and quiltmaking.

6. MEASURING TAPE

If you buy only one measuring device, an extra-long measuring tape (such as quilter's tape) will cover almost all instances.

7. FABRIC MARKER

This is a pen that can be used to draw on fabric, like a modern-day tailor's chalk (although you can still use chalk, if you prefer it). I like to use water-soluble fabric markers, as the ink can then be washed out when you have finished sewing the project, but you can purchase heat-erasable pens too if you like the idea of ironing out the markings instead. Always test the pen first on a scrap of the fabric to be used, so you can check how well it erases.

8. FABRIC GLUE

For temporary fixing where tacking / basting stitches won't do, fabric glue will do the job nicely. Most fabric glue is just the same as normal glue – all you really need to have is a non-toxic, water-washable, clear-drying glue.

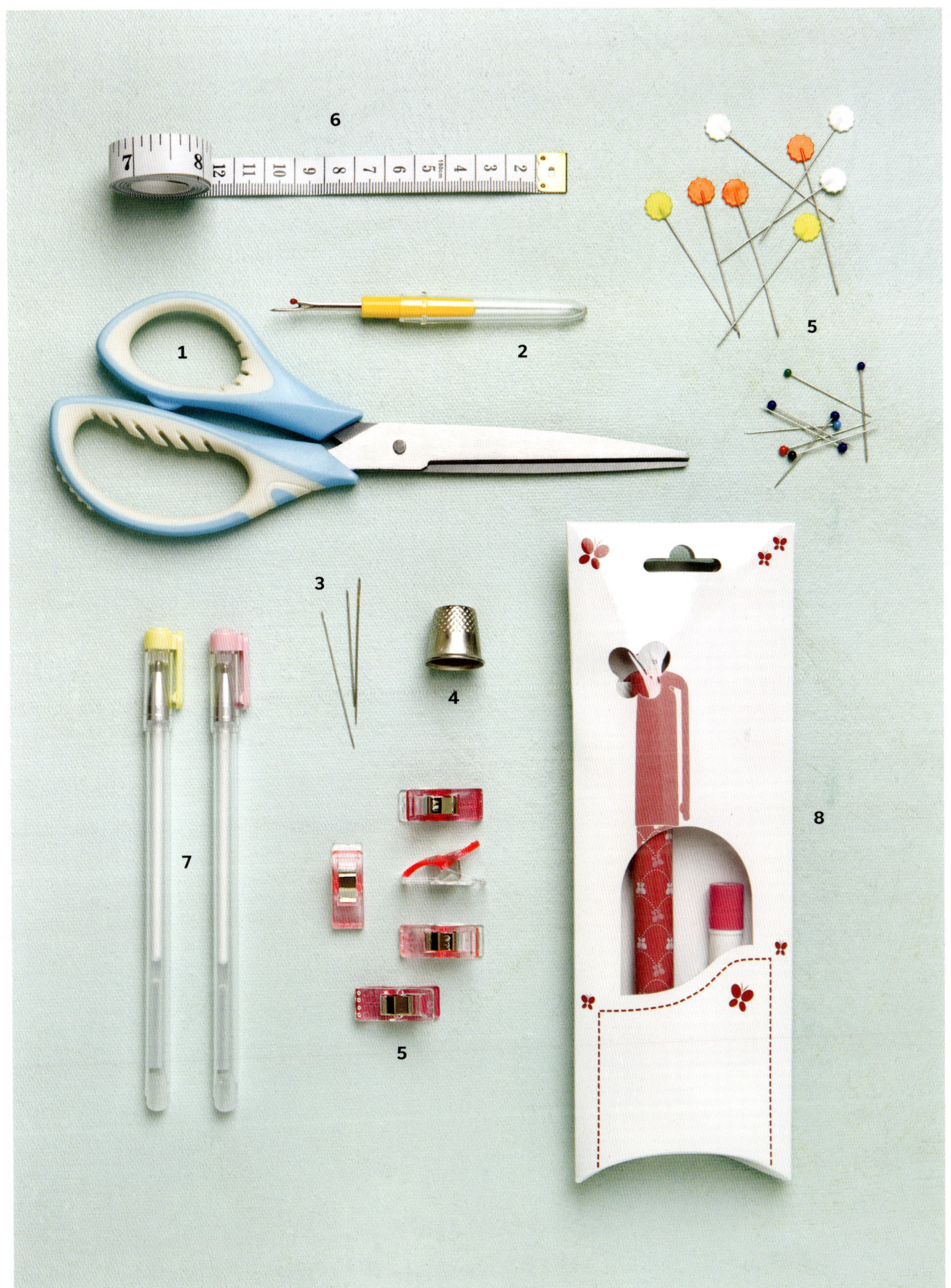
6
5
1
2
5
3
4
8
7
5

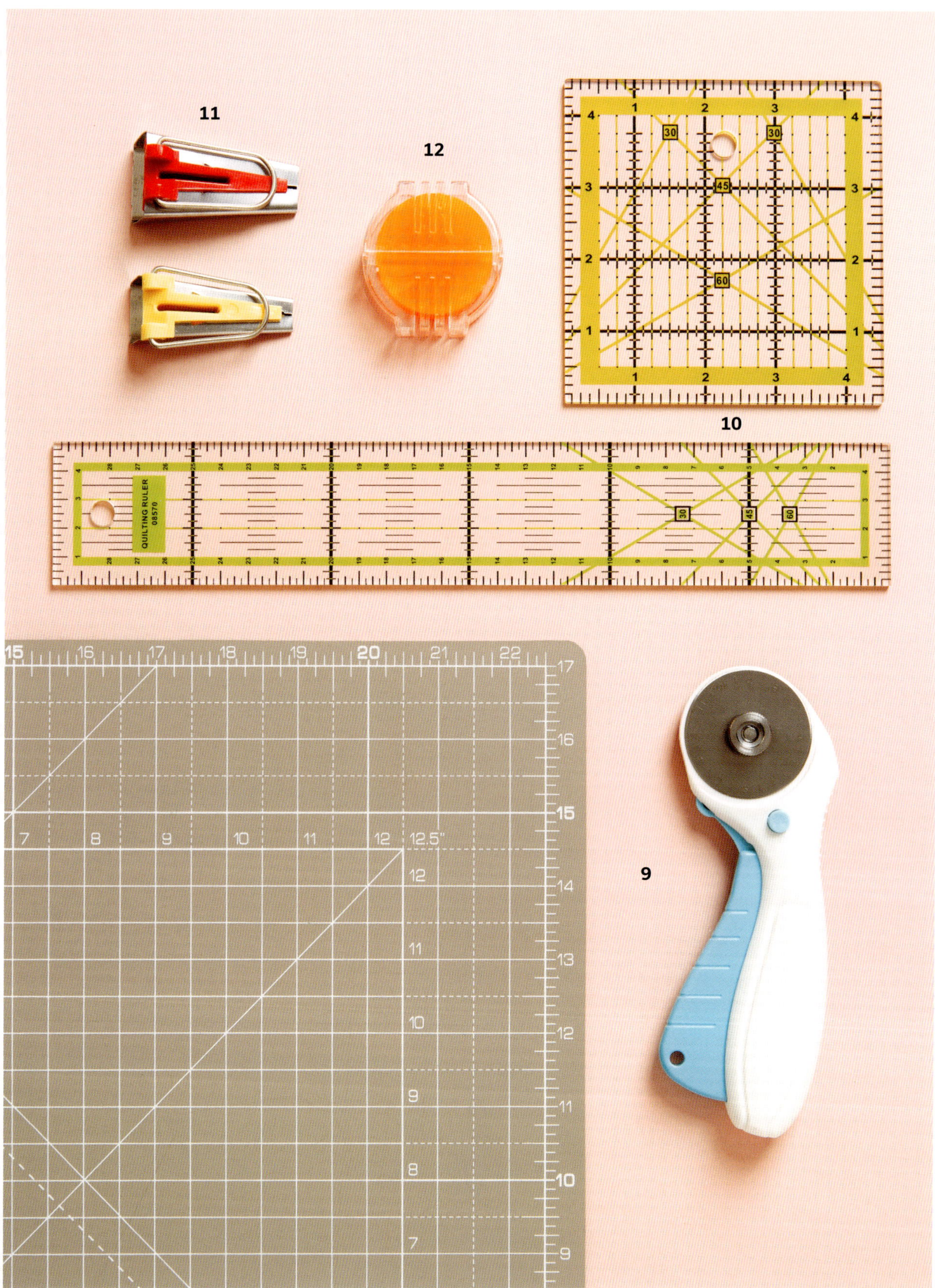
11
12
10
QUILTING RULER
08570
9

ADVANCED SEWING TOOLS

9. ROTARY CUTTER & SELF-HEALING CUTTING MAT

These are expensive but worth buying for accuracy and also for cutting multiple fabrics at once. If you ever decide to go down the quilting route (and there are some tasty makes later on in the book) this little set will be moved up to the cannot-possibly-live-without category.

10. QUILTING RULERS

If you get into quiltmaking, acrylic rulers will be your best friend, thanks to their accuracy and the angles printed on them too. As they're designed to be used with a rotary cutter, they're much thicker than ordinary rulers; do not use regular rulers with a rotary cutter, as the latter will easily cut through these.

11. BIAS TAPE MAKER

It's possible to make bias tape (more on this later) without a bias tape maker, but this will make the process much simpler. See page 59 for details.

12. THREAD CONDITIONER

It might seem odd to recommend beeswax in your sewing kit, but until you have wrestled with a piece of thread that is tangling and behaving awfully, you will not see the point. A wax block is used to condition the thread before hand-sewing, and this stops tangles and makes the thread stronger. Your wax block could be a lump of an old candle, as long as it is colourless and natural beeswax.

SEWING MACHINES

You do not need a top-of-the-range machine to begin with – you just need one that will allow you to sew a straight stitch and a zigzag stitch, and one that can take a couple of different feet. If you need a general overview of the kind of features you can find on a sewing machine, take a look at pages 22–23.

There are two main kinds of sewing machine: mechanical and computerized. Mechanical machines offer fewer features, but tend to be cheaper to buy and fix. If you're into lots of stitching possibilities down the line, and more versatility with stitch widths and more, computerized machines are perfect for the job: they usually come with around 20 different stitches built in, and the feet can be shifted up, down and side to side at the tap of a button. There are some cons, however; computerized machines tend to be more expensive, and repairs can be costly too.

Sewing machines always come with a universal / standard foot, but you can also purchase extra feet for your machine to serve special purposes. The key three feet to ask about when buying are a walking foot (for quilting), a zipper foot (for zips and binding) and a darning foot (for free-motion embroidery, known as 'FME' for short). Don't worry about how to use these at the moment; these special feet will come up as we go.

When it comes to machine needles, I recommend Prym or Schmetz as I have been using them for my whole sewing life. The best sizes to go for when sewing cotton fabrics are 'universal' – size 80/12 or 90/14. The general rule is the heavier the fabric, the thicker the needle – which makes sense when you think about it.

Universal / standard foot

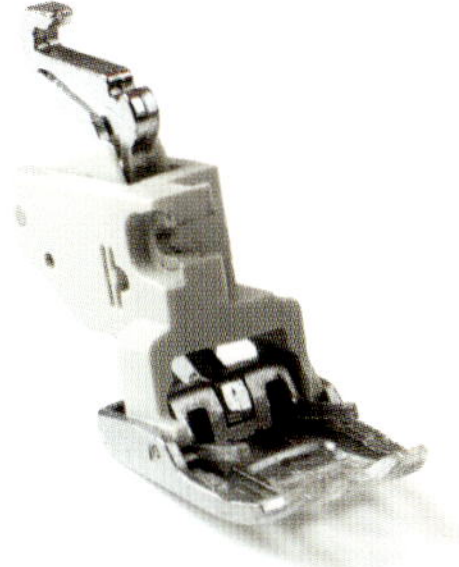
Walking (even / dual feed) foot

Zipper foot

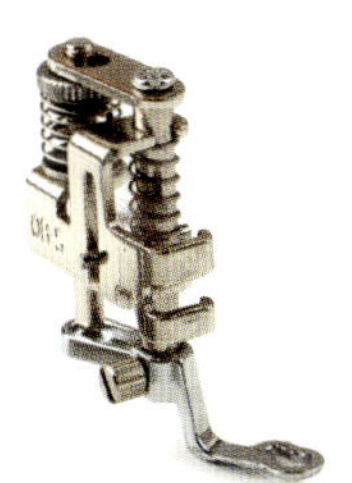
Darning foot

FABRICS

WHAT TO BUY AS A BEGINNER

The world of fabric is vast and the choices on offer can be overwhelming if you're a beginner to sewing. So, let's keep it simple.

First of all, this book is not about sewing clothes or wearables, so that rules out man-made fibres, stretch fabrics, novelty fabrics (the sort featuring knit or sequins) and anything that you might reach for to make evening wear. Our part of the fabric shop deals with **quilting cottons (1)**, pure **cotton (2)**, **canvas (3)**, **linen (4)**, real **leather** or **cork fabric (5)**, and **wool felt (6)**.

Woven fabrics – like cotton, canvas and linen – are not only the easiest fabrics to stitch with, but they tend to be more economical and come in a wide range of colours and prints. Haberdashery and fabric stores often have sales for quilt cottons, so keep an eye out for these and buy them for a future project. Cotton and linen are considered light- to medium-weight fabrics, ideal for most projects; canvas is a heavy-weight fabric, so is best used for projects that need sturdiness like bags and curtains.

Wool felt is another fabric that's beginner friendly, thanks to its stiffness and the fact it has no grain (see page 14 for more information about what this is), which means you can cut pieces from it in any direction. I like to buy heathered wool felt, as this has a lovely flecked appearance. I don't recommend nylon craft felt as it can wear down over time and doesn't look very nice either.

The one thing that you might not know is that you can buy felt by the metre or yard, as well as in smaller cuts; so, if you decide you like working with this material, you can invest in this and give yourself more options. Wool felt comes in different thicknesses, and which one you choose will depend on what the pattern requires and what your sewing machine can cope with.

To add some luxury to your projects, you can introduce small **leather** elements. If you're purchasing real leather, clothing weight as opposed to upholstery grade is perfect. Look out for clothing-industry scrap leather bags, as these are not only good quality but more economical. If you don't want to use real leather for ethical reasons, I recommend using **cork fabric** rather than faux leather; faux leather is tricky to sew with, and can wear badly very quickly.

Fabric anatomy

I mentioned the word 'woven' a little earlier and it is the next subject up for consideration. Most fabric (felt and leather being the exceptions from our list) is woven. Woven fabric is made by weaving long, fine threads together. The vertical ones are known as '**warp threads**', and the horizontal ones are called '**weft threads**'. These interlace to create a **grain**. The **straight grain** therefore runs two ways - up and down (**lengthwise grain**), and across the fabric (sometimes known as the **cross grain**).

Unless stated otherwise in the pattern or on the template, **fabric should always be cut on the straight grain**. This is because the straight grain has no stretch. If you pull the fabric from the top and bottom edges, and left- and right-hand sides, you'll see how these barely move.

However, if you pull the fabric at opposite corners (i.e. diagonally), you'll see how there is some stretch. This diagonal is called the **bias**. The stretch in the bias can mean that cut fabric distorts badly - mind you, you can use this stretchiness to your advantage sometimes too; for example, it is the bias stretch that allows bias binding to fit around rounded corners.

The easiest way to find the straight grain is to look for the **selvedges / selvages**. These are the 'finished' edges on the fabric made during the manufacturing process - i.e. edges that have been industrially hemmed or bound to prevent the fabric from fraying. The easiest way to spot a selvedge / selvage is it often has information about the fabric printed on it or it's perforated, and runs along the whole length of the fabric. The selvedges / selvages should always be trimmed off before sewing.

There is a '**right side**' and a '**wrong side**' to fabric too, and you need to know this terminology when you're reading a pattern. Put simply, the right side (**RS**) is the prettier side, and the one that we want to see when we are finished. The wrong side (**WS**) is the back of the fabric, and is usually unprinted. Most of the time, in order for your project's seams to be hidden on the inside, you'll need to sew your fabric pieces 'right sides together' (i.e. the wrong sides will be facing you when you sew) then turn them through so the right side is facing out again. Good quality solid fabrics will often have no 'wrong side', so either side can be used as the right side. However, it is a good idea to examine them in good light to make sure.

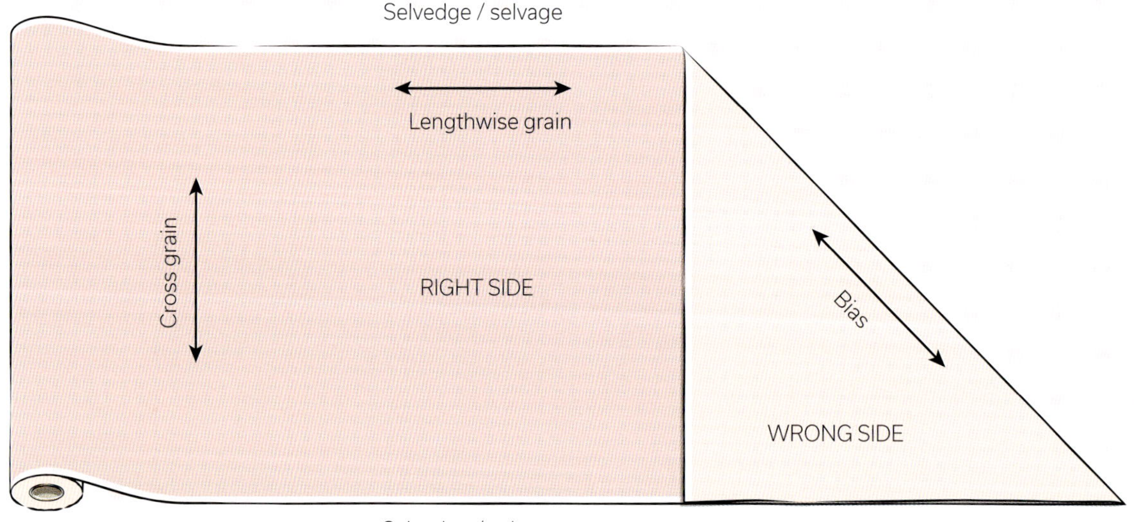

HOW TO BUY

The first rule is to buy the best quality fabric that you can afford – it will last longer and usually washes well – and from a known brand if you can. I know that we are often led off the path of virtue by telling ourselves that 'you are only paying for the name' but that is not the complete truth. The better brands care about their product, and they are very aware that it is not worth cutting corners when it comes to quality and, with it, their reputation.

Good-quality fabrics do come with a higher price tag, but if you're clever with your purchases you can buy them in smaller quantities, and build your stash over time. Quilting cottons are great early purchases, particularly pre-cuts like Fat Quarters (50.75 x 45.75cm / 20 x 18in), which are not only on the cheaper side but their 'fat' shape goes an awfully long way. With one Fat Quarter you can make a pillow or a large mat, and cut nearly 7m (7½yd) of bias binding; two Fat Quarters can be turned into a bag, too.

Do you worry about choosing colours or patterns? You can buy coordinated Fat Quarter bundles from most sewing outlets, and these are great when you're starting out: a lot of thought has gone into choosing fabrics for the bundle, and the selection is designed to be used together. You can use these bundles as jumping-off points too – if you combine them intelligently with bolts of coordinating plain fabrics (called '**solids**') or '**blenders**' (fabrics with a subtle print – think somewhere between strong prints and solids), you can make many more projects for much less than you think.

If you are flying solo with your fabric choices, I have a formula that works very well. Begin with your 'hero print'; this is a printed fabric that you love, and has a theme that attracts you. Now look at it really well. Squint. Which colour is the most dominant? This is what you'll use for your solid fabric. Which colour only appears a teensy bit? That last colour is what we will use to choose a blender. Choosing this way means that your solid and blender fabrics will not argue with the hero print. If you chose your dominant colour as the blender, it would swamp everything completely.

LOOKING AFTER FABRIC

Try to store fabric away from direct sunlight in a box or cupboard. Even the best quality fabrics can fade and some colours are worse for this than others.

What about washing? Whether to pre-wash your fabric before stitching with it is hotly debated in the sewing community. If you're sewing clothes (not covered in this book), it's worth doing in case of shrinkage and colour changes. When it comes to sewing accessories, like the projects in this book, I tend not to pre-wash; I have never found it necessary in more than 40 years of sewing, although I am quite possibly lazy...

Always iron your fabrics before cutting and sewing with them, to get rid of creases and folds that would lead to inaccuracies. This includes any scraps of fabric that you're going to use in projects, not just brand-new lengths of fabric or pre-cuts.

Pre-cuts

These are fabrics cut to a specific size by a manufacturer, and are often associated with quiltmaking. Fat Quarters are the most well-known and popular pre-cuts. A sister of the Fat Quarter is the Fat Eighth, which is half the size of a Fat Quarter. I like to have a few Fat Eighths in my stash, as they are great for smaller projects and accents. You can also buy smaller pre-cuts like Charm Packs and Jelly Rolls, but these are more useful for quiltmakers.

INTERFACING

Interfacing is a bit less interesting than the flashy fabrics that we see every day, but it is oh so important. Usually I open the subject of interfacing by comparing it to decent undergarments: just as a good bra will change the look of a dress, great interfacing will lift your projects from a home-made to professional finish.

In short, interfacing is a special kind of fabric that's applied to the back of fabrics (or between layers of fabrics) to give the finished item a soft structure. Not using interfacing at all, or using really cheap, questionable interfacing, is the equivalent of that bra that is held together with electrical tape and chewing gum – pointless.

There are different kinds of interfacing readily available to buy in bricks-and-mortar stores and online, by several brands and each kind serving a slightly different purpose. Knowing which to invest in can be overwhelming, but the great news is that interfacing really can be kept to a minimum. So you buy only what's required, I'll take you through my favourites that I cannot sew without.

- Number one is a **light-weight sew-in foam interfacing (1)**, and I like to use Style-Vil by Vlieseline®. This is about 5mm (¼in) thick, and I use it anywhere I want serious structure. It's also washable too. I cannot imagine making a bag without it.

  To attach sew-in foam interfacing, you will need to cut a panel that's about 2cm (¾in) larger all around than the panel of fabric to be interfaced. Lay the fabric wrong side down onto the foam and pin well. Using a very narrow tacking / basting stitch (set the stitch length on your machine to the longest one possible) and keeping a gentle tension on the fabric panel, sew all around the perimeter. Trim the foam back to the edge of the fabric panel.
- Another interfacing that I use a lot is a **medium-weight fusible cotton interlining (2)**. My favourite is G740 by Vlieseline®, which sounds like a major and very important political summit, but is in fact a very useful interfacing. It has a rough (glue) side and a smooth top side; the glue (rough) side goes against the wrong side of the fabric and you can then iron it on. Get to know which side is which really well because if you put it the wrong way up your iron will not thank you for it!

  G740 is the thinnest of woven interfacings and it has a similar weight to cheesecloth, so does not significantly add to the weight of the fabric but adds a light level of structure to the item to which it's fused. I use it for pockets on bags, but it's mainly useful for stabilizing fabrics which fray excessively.

2

1

3

- Next in line is a **low-loft fusible wadding / batting (3)** – and for this I use H630 also by Vlieseline®. Wadding / batting is used mainly in quiltmaking (for the squishy layer between the front and back of the quilt), with 'low loft' meaning this layer is on the very thin end of the volume range. However, this light-weight wadding / batting is great for adding soft but voluminous structure to projects. Here again, the rough side is the glue side, and this product is easiest to work with if the interfacing's fleecy side is facing *down* onto the ironing board, then your fabric panel to be interfaced is laid on top, its wrong side facing down and over the glue side of the interfacing. Press with an iron to fuse, then trim to the size and shape of the fabric panel.
- **Iron-on, paper-backed adhesive web (4)** is worth a mention, and I use Bondaweb by Vlieseline®. This is great for appliqué, like the fish for our storage cube (see page 84). It is really simple to use too.

  Firstly, using the necessary template (the pattern will explain which one to use), draw the motif onto the smooth / paper side of the web then cut it out, leaving a narrow border. Place the shape rough (glue) side down onto the wrong side of the desired fabric piece. Press to fuse with a hot iron. Cut out each piece precisely then peel the paper away – this will now make the fabric shape fusible. Lay the fabric shape onto the project in the desired spot, then press with an iron to secure when you are happy.
- **Light-weight non-woven fusible interlining (5)**, such as Decovil I Light by Vlieseline®, is one of those really useful fusible interfacings. It has the weight and feel of a thin leather or vinyl, and because it's non-woven it has no stretch, making it great for adding soft structure and stability to fabric.
- Finally, the most-used interfacing is... wait for it... a **cotton-polyester mix medium-weight sew-in wadding / batting (6)** – I use 279 Cotton Mix 80 /20 by Vlieseline® (I need to speak to Vlieseline about some of these names!). Like H630, this is closer to a quilt wadding / batting than an interfacing as such, and similarly this adds a lovely bit of volume to projects as well as structure.

  To use, cut a piece that is about 2.5cm (1in) larger all around than the panel of fabric to which you're attaching it. Once you've stitched, you can trim the wadding / batting to size.

THREADS

You may have the following questions when you're deciding what kind of threads to buy: should I buy a top brand or will something cheaper do just as well? Or will everything that I've sewn fall apart immediately if I purchase a discount brand?

I never buy top brands of thread. Never. Sometimes they are sent to me, and I really love using them, but that is usually the end of the line. Simply put, they eat too much into my budget and I have never found them necessary. However, I don't buy cheap and nasty either. Cheap threads can be difficult to sew with, but risk snapping too.

To find a thread that sits between expensive and cheap, look for threads at a sewing shop that's reputable, then take a look at the selection of colours offered too. This second point alone seems to ensure that the quality is good – if your thread only comes in brightest red, brightest yellow and brightest blue, it is not usually a sign that much thought has gone into its manufacture. However, if you can see more muted options on offer, that's usually a sign that someone cares about the product enough to create something more attractive.

If your budget is restrictive, it's worth keeping an eye on the good brands when they're sold at a discount.

Always choose a colour thread that's as close to the colour of your fabric as possible. You will be amazed at how much this simple tip will lift your sewing immediately. Nothing looks more 'homemade' than the wrong thread or the same one (white for example) used on everything. When you are starting out, buy thread each time you buy fabric; after a while, you'll have built a small stash with enough colours in it to suit any fabric combination.

Threads carry a number to let you know their weight, but this is not always easy to find – and some brands don't have it at all. Here again, I opt for a universal thread weight for cotton fabrics, and I tend to sew pretty much everything from bags to quilts with it. I sew denim and leather with a universal weight thread that a dressmaker might use too.

This is a bit of a hot take, because we are supposed to worry about using certain threads for particular fabrics. But I don't, and in 40 years of sewing I have not. My best advice? Sew a sample of the stitch that you want to use on the fabric that you have chosen with the needle and thread and see how it behaves with *your* machine. If everything looks good, you are off to the races!

The only time that you might have to think again about thread weights is if you are sewing a *lot* of leather (rather than just one or two trims), and you are having enormous trouble with skipped stitches and your machine generally behaving badly. The general rule is to go for a heavier weight of thread for a heavier weight of fabric. Note that the needle will need to be changed too.

HABERDASHERY, HARDWARE AND TRIMS

Every now and then, a sewing pattern calls for something a little extra.

Let's start with **zips**. These come in a few different permutations, and the most likely ones seen everyday are either plastic or metal. I tend to choose metal for zips that will be seen (the outsides of bags, for example), and plastic for more hidden closures like lapped zips and inside pockets. That is my personal choice and you can, of course, go for a totally different combination.

In a similar aesthetical vein, I choose wooden buttons over plastic, and cotton webbing for bag handles over nylon every time. I like the look and feel of the more substantial natural fibres.

There are a few patterns where you will be called on to make a choice about **trims**. Although budget is an obvious consideration, there are so many worthwhile options in the cheaper areas that you will still be spoiled for choice. When I started sewing with my Nana (last century) you could not buy anywhere near the variety that is on sale now. Get to know what is available, experiment, and see what sings to you.

Nothing lifts a project like quality **metal hardware**! This is something I am ready to defend to the last. Rivets, D-rings, rectangle rings, studs and fancy closures all come under this heading, and they are a wonderful addition to your projects, particularly for bagmaking.

If you opt for a decent brand, the tools required to fit them will come with the hardware in question; all you need to do is grab a hammer from the shed. Cheaper brands do offer some advantages – often the tools will be available in a larger pack. It is worthwhile investing in a hole punch (holes are needed for many things) and a small hammer, if you don't have one already.

Not only is it used in one of the projects in this book (see page 50), but worth always having in your sewing stash is **woven elastic** – the kind you can find in waistbands for skirts and trousers. I like to keep a few widths of elastic in my stash, some in black and some in white, for new projects or to replace old elastic (as it can lose its stretch over a period of time). My favourite elastic widths are 5mm (¼in) and 1.5cm (½in) wide, as they can be used for most projects.

A book about sewing has to mention **binding**. This is a folded strip of fabric tape used mainly for covering the raw edges of fabric, but can be used to make piping (see below). You can buy or make binding tape yourself (see page 59 for more on the latter). The purchased varieties, while totally adequate, are a bit of a let-down in terms of style. The quality of the fabric never feels very nice, and you have to accept the colours and widths on offer. It won't surprise you to know that I make my binding most of the time, and I'll show you how to do this later in the book. Not only is making binding easier than you think, it allows you to match your binding exactly to your project – giving a much more professional finish.

Our final piece of haberdashery is **piping**. Used for the pillow edging on page 94, piping is essentially binding tape wrapped around a length of cord that is then stitched around the edge of a project, creating a stylish 3D edging. Like binding, you can buy piping but it's just as easy to make your own and means you can colour match it to the item you're sewing too. Take a look at page 92 for more information about how to make piping.

Glossary

Sewing has a lot of terms, and these can be overwhelming to learn when you're starting out. Here is a list of all the key jargon that you'll encounter as you read through this book.

Backing fabric A term used mostly in quilting, this is the bottom fabric in a 'quilt sandwich' (see below), and faces right side out.

Bagging out This is simply another way to finish an item of sewing. It refers to placing the pieces to be sewn right sides together, sewing around the edge and leaving a turning gap (see opposite). You then turn the item to the right side through the turning gap, close the turning gap and press the edges. There is a bit more to it than this, of course, in an actual pattern; extra processes are explained as and when you need them.

Binding Folded strip of fabric (usually made up of multiple lengths of fabric joined together) that is wrapped around the raw edges of a project to hide them and prevent them from fraying.

Blender A blender fabric features a subtle print, and is included in a collection to complement the hero fabric. It is a supporting act and you can use it knowing that the project will look well put together and not too busy.

Bobbin This is the little spool in a sewing machine that holds the bottom thread. As you sew, it links together with the top thread to form the stitches. The position of the bobbin case (where the bobbin sits in the machine) varies in different sewing machine models.

Directional fabric This refers to a pattern which has a definite top and bottom, and it matters if you use it the 'wrong' way up. An example might be a fabric with people's faces, animals, birds or scenes. Sometimes this will mean you need to buy slightly more fabric to cut out the various pieces of your project, as you cannot be creative with the cutting direction. You have to work with the fabric.

Grain If you're working with woven fabrics like cotton, you'll encounter a 'grain' – these are the vertical and horizontal threads that make up the fabric. Grain is important when sewing; more on this on page 14!

Guide bar This fits into the walking (even- / dual-feed) foot to help you to space the stitches when sewing parallel lines of quilting.

Pinked edges This sounds like dark magic, but in fact what it means is to use pinking shears to finish the edge of the fabric so that it will not fray quite so easily. Pinking shears are special, bulky scissors with zigzag or scalloped blades, instead of the usual flat edges that we see on normal scissors. This automatically cuts the fabric with either a scallop or zigzag pattern. Using these scissors is always a good move if you're working with slightly looser weave fabrics (I'm looking at you, linen), which need special handling.

Press This is literally pressing the area (usually a seam) with an iron for a few seconds, without moving the iron around.

Quilting Decorative stitching that also secures the layers in a 'quilt sandwich' (see below) together.

Quilt sandwich The layers making up a quilt: backing fabric, wadding / batting and quilt top.

Quilt top The top layer of a 'quilt sandwich' (see above), which is decorative as this is the side of the quilt on display. Classic quilt tops have a patchwork design – i.e. made from lots of little cut fabric shapes stitched together.

Raw edge This is the very edge of your cut fabric. If an instruction says 'raw edges matching', it means align the very edges of your fabric pieces. This does assume you've cut your fabric accurately and neatly!

Reverse stitch(ing) Sometimes known as 'backstitching' or 'back-tacking', this is a way of securing a stitch by locking it with another stitch over the top. Your machine will have a function to do this and it is best to check the manual for details.

Right side (RS) This is a term used to describe the 'front' of the fabric, or the side you wish to appear on the outside of an item.

Seam This is your line of stitching securing your fabric pieces together. A seam can be straight, curved or go round a whole project.

Seam allowance Shortened to 'SA' in most patterns, this is the distance between the edge of your fabric and the seam. This distance not only makes the seam neat on the right side of the fabric, it also keeps your stitch line away from the raw edge of the fabric, where it can fray and unravel. Unless stated otherwise in the pattern, a 5mm (¼in) seam allowance should be used every time you sew.

Sewing within the seam allowance The seam allowances used in this book are all 5mm (¼in) wide and, conveniently, this is the width of many presser feet. Sewing within the seam allowance refers to stitches or a line of stitching at say, 2–3mm (⅛in). This line of stitching or stitches will then serve a purpose (extra strength, for example) but be invisible in the final product.

Solid fabric A term used mainly in quiltmaking, this is basically plain, one-coloured fabric with no pattern printed on it.

Tacking / basting This describes the process of holding pieces of fabric together with temporary stitches. Tacking / basting stitches are usually longer than your regular stitch length to make them easier to remove later. For more details, see page 26.

Top thread This links with your bobbin thread to make a stitch. The top thread is your 'main' thread, and can also sit in slightly different places on your machine, depending on the model.

Turning gap This is a gap deliberately left in a seam to allow you to turn the item either right side out or wrong side out, depending on the instructions.

Turn(ing) through The process of turning the project through a deliberate gap in the seam, either so the right side is facing out or to turn it inside out.

Turn(ing) under Fold over the edge of the fabric, usually so the wrong sides are facing.

Wadding / batting The padded middle layer of a 'quilt sandwich' (see opposite), adding warmth, weight and drape to a quilt.

Wrong side (WS) This is a term used to describe the 'back' of the fabric, or the side you wish to appear on the inside of an item.

Getting started

This section is all about the basics you need to know before you get started on your sewing journey. Once learned, you can turn your hand to many sewing projects, in this book and in the future.

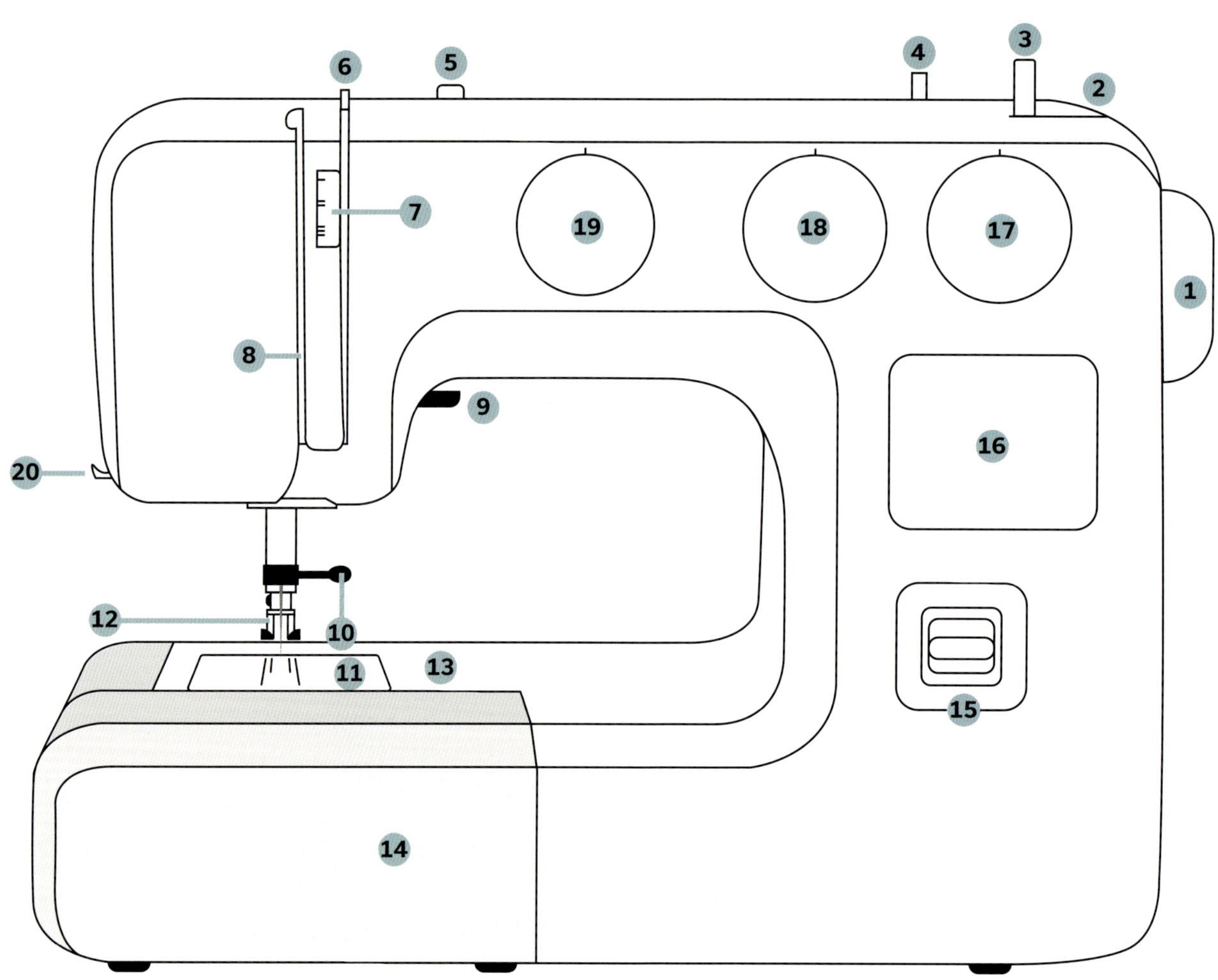

SEWING MACHINE ANATOMY

It is beyond the scope of any book to go through the ins and outs of your specific sewing machine, as they're all different; so, I recommend taking a look at your own machine's manual before you start sewing. It's also worth searching online for videos on your specific brand, to master the basics. However, here are the most common features you'll find on a sewing machine:

1. **Hand wheel** Turn this to lift or lower the needle. Always turn the wheel towards you (counter-clockwise); turning it away from you slightly (clockwise) is fine for thread jams, but doing this consistently can throw off internal timings in the machine. Sometimes the hand wheel includes a setting or button that enables you to change the machine setting to winding a bobbin.
2. **Bobbin winder stop** A small disc on some sewing machines, built in to stop the bobbin winding when it is full of thread.
3. **Spool holder** A long peg for the top thread (i.e. the main reel of thread you're sewing with).
4. **Bobbin winder** A small peg for an empty bobbin to sit on, when you're winding it with thread.
5. **Bobbin winding tension disc** The thread from the spool runs around this when you're winding the bobbin, to add tension.
6. **Thread take-up lever** The top thread runs through the thread guide and over this lever or hook, to maintain thread tension when sewing.
7. **Tension control** Where the button is placed varies from machine to machine. The dial controls the tension of the top thread on the spool; the smaller the number, the greater the tension, and vice versa.
8. **Thread guide** The top thread is threaded through this curved channel to hold the thread in place, aligning it correctly for sewing.
9. **Presser foot lever** This raises and lowers the presser foot, either moving it out of the way or holding the fabric in place for sewing.
10. **Needle clamp** Loosen or tighten to remove and swap a needle.
11. **Needle plate** Where the feed dogs poke out (see page 80); the plate also often includes handy measurements for seam allowances. Depending on the machine, you may see a **top-loading bobbin compartment** sitting close to the needle plate.
12. **Presser foot** Universal / standard foot shown; can be removed to change to another foot.
13. **Sewing machine 'free arm'** When revealed (usually by removing the accessory compartment), this is handy for sewing tubular shapes.
14. **Removable accessory compartment** Slides off to reveal a hidden compartment where you can store sewing machine accessories. It also allows you to reveal the 'free arm'. On some models, removing the accessory compartment gives you access to a **front-loading bobbin compartment**.
15. **Reverse button or lever** Allows you to reverse stitch or backstitch (i.e. sew backwards), to secure stitches before cutting the thread.
16. **Stitch reference** Sometimes included on machines, this lists all the stitches the machine can sew, with a corresponding number. This is either printed directly on the machine, or on a sticker.
17. **Stitch selector** This is a dial or computer screen where you change the stitch your machine is sewing.
18. **Stitch length selector** This is a dial or button that enables you to increase or decrease the length of the stitch. This is important in sewing, as the stitch length required varies from fabric to fabric: if the stitch length is too short it will pucker the fabric; if it is too long, the seam will not hold together properly.
19. **Stitch width selector** Not all machines have this as a feature, but it's useful for decorative stitches, or zigzag and overlock / serge stitches. This is a dial or button that allows you to adjust the width of a stitch.
20. **Thread cutter** High-end sewing machines feature a button that perfectly cuts the thread for you once you've finished sewing on the machine. However, most basic models feature a little cutter at the side of the machine for you to manually cut the thread with.

SEWING A SEAM

This is the most fundamental technique on your sewing journey. You will take two pieces of fabric, place them right sides together and sew!

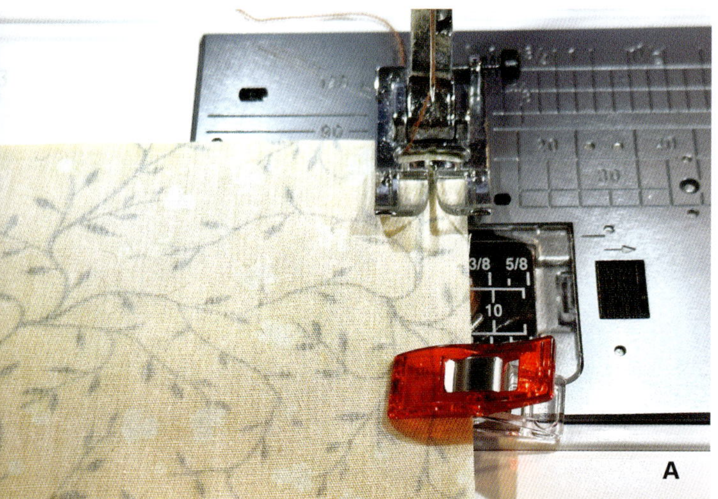

SEWING IN A STRAIGHT LINE

1 Place two pieces of fabric right sides (RS) together, making sure the edges you'll sew along align – i.e. one fabric doesn't overlap the other, their edges match. Then, temporarily secure them with pins or clips. If you're using pins, make sure they're perpendicular to the fabric, with the pin heads beyond the raw edges of the fabric.

2 Raise the presser foot. Place the pinned pieces of fabric onto the sewing machine needle plate, under the presser foot. If your needle plate has measurements on it (these are different seam allowance widths), adjust your fabric to your chosen measurement (**A**). When you sew, the machine will gently pull the fabric behind the presser foot (so backwards); bear this is mind also when deciding where to position your fabric under the foot.

3 Lower the presser foot, set your stitch and stitch length on the machine, then sew from top to bottom. Remove the pins or clips as you sew so that you do not run over them; sewing over them can break the needle. Assuming your fabric is cut straight, and you sew neatly, you should have a straight line of stitching from the beginning to the end of the seam.

SEWING A CORNER

1 When it comes to sewing corners of shapes like squares and rectangles, stitch towards the edge of the fabric then stop the same distance as your seam allowance (SA).

2 Ensuring the needle is still in the fabric, lift the presser foot and rotate the fabric in the new direction with your hands (**B**). It's super important to have the needle down when you do this because that allows you to 'keep your place' and sew precisely where you left off.

3 Lower the presser foot once you've finished rotating the fabric, then continue to sew as described above.

NOTCHING AND CLIPPING

Where you have curves in your joined fabric pieces, you'll need to cut a little into the seam allowances for the fabrics sit neatly when turned through. Whether you should notch or clip usually depends on the curve – typically notching is for convex curves, and clipping is for concave curves and unusual shapes.

Warning

With either of these techniques, it's vital you do not cut into your stitching – you should cut about 2–3mm (⅛in) shy of the seam, so there's no risk of snipping into your stitching.

Notching is the removal of little V-shaped chunks in the seam allowance, usually around a convex curve. When the project is turned the right way out, these little notches will knit together.

Clipping is making little snips in the seam allowance. This allows the fabric to spread out when stretched around a curve.

PRESSING A SEAM

Almost all sewing patterns will tell you to press the seam allowance after sewing. This not only neatens the seam on the wrong side of the fabric, but reduces bulk in the seam too. Pressing a seam open (i.e. like the pages of an open book), as shown, should be your default unless stated otherwise in the instructions.

1 Sharply run your fingernail along the seam to open it out before pressing. I recommend doing this with longer seams, which tend to keep collapsing in on themselves otherwise.

2 To press your seam allowance open properly, and secure it, simply press a hot iron down the centre of the seam. Do not move the iron round like you do when ironing clothes, as this will distort the seam allowance; you need only hold the iron over the seam for a few seconds, then repeat along the seam.

MACHINE STITCHES

The two machine stitches used the most in this book, and the ones that will get you through pretty much any sewing project, are straight stitch and zigzag stitch.

Make sure your sewing machine is set up before you begin – take a look at your machine's sewing manual for guidance. For your top thread (i.e. the reel of the thread that, literally, sits on top of your machine), always use a colour that matches your fabric. This is also important with your bobbin thread if it will be seen – for example, when top-stitching. Sometimes it is necessary for the bobbin thread and the main top thread to be different colours to match the individual colours of fabric. The main thing is that they are the same weight of thread.

I am deliberately using a contrasting colour for the photographs in this section, so you can see the stitching more easily.

Bobbin

This is a small, cylindrical spool that fits into the machine under the needle plate, and which the 'bottom' thread is wound around. When in motion, the machine's threaded needle (which uses the 'top' thread) catches the thread from this bobbin, and combined they allow the sewing machine to make a stitch.

A

B

STRAIGHT STITCH

A straight stitch is exactly what it sounds like! A sewing machine will sew straight stitches closely together in a row, making a secure, neat line.

Straight stitches (and all of the stitches on your machine) can be lengthened or shortened – check your sewing machine manual for details. But why would you need to do this? For two reasons:

First, the weight of the fabric dictates the stitching length you'll use. Typically, light-weight fabrics need shorter stitches to prevent puckering; heavy-weight fabrics need longer stitches to stop the seams being too stiff.

Second, it depends on how secure you want your stitches to be. Shorter stitches are less likely to come undone (**A**). Techniques like free-motion embroidery (see page 80) require the shortest stitch possible (length '0'). At the other end of the spectrum, the longest stitch on your machine is great for temporary stitches like tacking / basting (**B**), which need to be as easy as possible to unpick. Most of the time you'll want a medium-length straight stitch; typically this is the factory-set stitch on the machine.

ZIGZAG STITCH

This is a stitch that literally forms a zigzag pattern with the stitches. You can use it to finish the edges of seam allowances and stop the fabric fraying (see page 90); it's also useful for attaching trims like lace, which often sit right on the edge of an item and can't be secured with regular straight stitch.

A zigzag stitch can be adjusted in width as well as length. Wide zigzags can span a large area (great for attaching lace); narrow zigzags can be used to create a satin stitch infill effect, for a decorative purpose.

TOP-STITCH

Top-stitch simply refers to a line of stitching that is designed to be seen on the right side of whatever you are making. It's usually done close to a seam for both decorative and functional reasons.

If you're really worried about your stitches being on show, match your thread as closely to the fabric as possible; this way they won't stand out quite so much.

EDGE-STITCH

This is very similar to top-stitch, but the stitch line is sewn much closer to the seam – 2–3mm (1⁄8in) away – and typically a matching thread is used to make the stitches as invisible as possible. This is because it serves more of a functional purpose than top-stitching: either it is used to flatten a seam, giving it a crisp edge; or, when the stitch length is increased and then sewn within the seam allowance, it temporarily secures layers of fabric in place without adding bulk if more additions are to be sewn in later.

HAND STITCHES

Finally we come to hand stitching. While it may seem strange to include this in a book on machine sewing, there will be instances where you'll need to do a little hand sewing – from closing turning gaps to finishing off ends that will be visible on the front of your fabric. On these pages are some important hand stitches to know before diving into the techniques and projects later in this book.

WHIP STITCH

This is simplest hand stitch out there! I like to use it for securing one side of the binding to the back of a quilt, as it's super secure and quick to work. For a subtle appearance, use a matching thread and make your stitches as tiny as possible.

1 Thread your needle then condition the thread with beeswax as detailed in the tip box, right.

2 Bring the needle up through the back to the right side of the work – in my case, I'm bringing my needle up through the fold of the binding (**A**) – to bury the knot on the wrong side of the fabric.

3 Take the needle down directly opposite where it came out then bring the needle out again approximately 5mm (¼in) next to where it first came out; one stitch made, and the next stitch started (**B**). Continue in this way along the rest of the seam.

4 To finish, make a few tiny stitches on top of each other and then take the needle down through the centre of them and deep between the fabric layers. Pull on the thread very slightly and trim it close to the fabric. The end of the thread tail will then disappear inside the layers. If you have a particularly thick interfacing, you can use this to your advantage to bury the thread end.

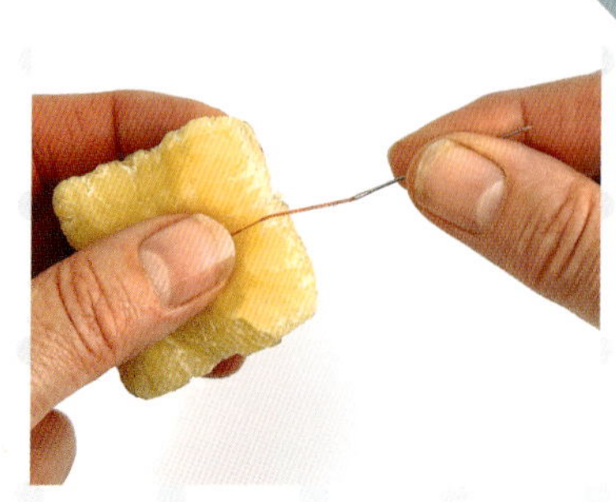

Using thread conditioner

After threading my needle and before hand sewing, I like to run my thread through the thread conditioner, as shown. The conditioner prevents tangles, reduces fraying, and allows the thread to glide more smoothly through the fabric.

A

B

LADDER STITCH

This stitch is worked from the right side of the fabric, and has a very subtle appearance – hence its other name, 'invisible stitch'.

Typically, ladder stitch is used to close turning gaps in sewing projects, particularly when it's not possible to sew from the wrong side of the fabric. When you are closing a turning gap, you will likely need to press the seam allowances of the opening to the wrong side, inside the item being sewn, before hand stitching.

1 Thread your needle and condition with wax as detailed in the tip box opposite. Bring the needle up through the back to the right side of the work – in my case, I'm bringing my needle up through the fold of the pressed seam allowance – to hide the knot between the fold on the wrong side of the fabric (**A**).

2 The working thread will be on the right side of the work now. On the opposite side of the gap where you came up, take the needle down and along the very edge of the fold – it should be parallel to it (**B**).

3 Take the needle down and up on the other side of the gap (i.e. the side you first brought up the needle), about 2–3mm (1/8in) farther along.

4 Repeat Steps 2 and 3 all along the gap, gently pulling the thread every few stitches to close the gap (**C**).

5 To finish, make a few tiny stitches on top of each other and then take the needle down through the centre of them and deep between the fabric layers. Pull on the thread very slightly and trim it close to the fabric. The end of the thread tail will then disappear between the layers on the wrong side of the fabric.

A

B

C

READING A PATTERN

When you first look at a sewing pattern, it may seem a little daunting as there are lots of different sections to read, some abbreviations and perhaps assumed knowledge.

But the good news is that most sewing patterns follow a similar format and are split into three sections:

- An introduction to the project and a photograph (or photographs) of the finished project.
- A section all about what materials you will need and what pieces you will need to cut, the stitches and techniques you will use, a list of abbreviations used within the pattern, and any project-specific notes.
- The written instructions for the project, which may include photos and/or diagrams.

It is vital that you read through a pattern before you buy your materials and begin sewing. This is so you can ensure that you have everything your need before you start, so that you don't need to go out and buy more materials; it's also so you can familiarize yourself with the making process, and avoid mistakes later down the line.

Here are some common terms that you may find within a pattern, and an explanation of what they mean.

1 SIZE

A pattern will always provide the measurements of the finished project, unless (like our reversible bowl cover on page 50 and our felt laptop sleeve on page 72) the project's size will vary depending on the item it's being made for.

2 SKILLS USED AND/OR DIFFICULTY LEVEL

This is the level of knowledge that is required to make the project. Usually this is written in words, but some designers or publishers may have a star or number rating system.

- **Easy or beginners:** Suitable for people who have recently learned to sew and know some sewing basics like how to cut fabric and sew a basic seam.
- **Confident beginners or intermediate:** Suitable for those with some sewing experience, who can sew more unusual shapes and fastenings.
- **Advanced:** Suitable for sewists who are very knowledgeable and experienced, and can follow complex instructions and create more involved items.

3 PATTERN NOTES

Most patterns will include notes to highlight seam allowances, to explain how the item is constructed, and to flag any unusual details. It's important to read this section carefully, so there are no surprises later!

4 YOU WILL NEED

All of the different things you will need to make your project are listed here, so that you can make sure you have everything required. If there are lots of fabrics, the publisher may describe them as Fabric 1, Fabric 2, and so on. Any extras will also be described here, such as special sewing machine feet or unusual sewing tools.

5 TO CUT

If some projects require the reader to cut their fabrics, interfacing or other materials into smaller pieces, some designers or publishers will have a separate cutting list before the instructions. The reason is that when you cut everything out in one go, you can work out the best possible usage for your fabric and prevent wastage. You will see this heading a great deal in quiltmaking patterns, as they often need you to cut out a lot of little pieces, and this can get out of hand if they're buried in the instructions!

Easy Trinket Tray

It is simply astounding how useful these little trays are around the house! I use mine in my sewing room for buttons and threads, my art room for small tools and things that I need to reach for again and again, and all around the rest of the house for safe-keeping things like keys, coins and the usual everyday bits and bobs.

SIZE 

24cm (9½in) square

SKILLS USED 

- Using fusible interfacing (page 34)
- Using a template (page 42)
- Making darts (page 42)
- Straight stitch (page 26)
- Sewing a seam (page 24)
- Turning through (page 35)
- Edge-stitch (page 27)
- Top-stitch (page 27)

PATTERN NOTES 

All seam allowances are 5mm (¼in) unless otherwise stated.

This tray can be easily resized up or down. Simply stick with a square and don't go much smaller than around 12.5cm (5in). The dart-corner template stays the same for all sizes.

YOU WILL NEED 

Fabric:

- 25cm (10in) square OR one Fat Quarter (56 x 45.75cm / 22 x 18in) of Fabric 1
- 25cm (10in) square OR one Fat Quarter (56 x 45.75cm / 22 x 18in) of Fabric 2

Interfacing:

- 56 x 45.75cm (22 x 18in, or one Fat Quarter) of light-weight fusible fleece – I've used H630 by Vlieseline®
- 56 x 45.75cm (22 x 18in, or one Fat Quarter) of light-weight non-woven fusible interfacing – I've used Decovil I Light by Vlieseline®

Everything else:

- Basic sewing tools (see page 8)
- Dart-corner template on page 119

TO CUT 

From Fabric 1 (if using a Fat Quarter):

- One 25cm (10in) square for the inside / top

From Fabric 2 (if using a Fat Quarter):

- One 25cm (10in) square for the outer / base

From the interfacing:

- One 25cm (10in) square from the light-weight fusible fleece
- One 25cm (10in) square from the very light-weight fusible interfacing

Techniques

and projects

Techniques

USING FUSIBLE INTERFACING

Almost every project in this book has interfacing of some sort. Interfacing adds some rigidity to a project, giving it that professional finish. With items that need only gentle structure, like the one coming up, turn to light-weight fusible (i.e. iron-on) interfacings. The best one for this project is a light-weight fusible fleece (I'm using H630 by Vlieseline®) and it is very simple to use.

Cut the interfacing to size and fuse it to the wrong side of the fabric with an iron, using the heat settings detailed on the packet instructions for the interfacing. If needed, trim the interfacing back to the size of the fabric.

ROUNDING CORNERS

If you want to introduce curved corners to your projects, as we will be for our upcoming mat, this is very simple to do: take a round object like a mug, side plate or even a tape reel that's roughly the size you wish your curve to be; lay it on your fabric, then use it as a template to draw around with your fabric marker.

SEWING AROUND A CURVE

This sounds pretty scary, but is in fact not much more difficult than sewing a straight seam. This is especially true if the curve is a nice gentle one. The larger the round shape, the gentler the curve will be. If you're choosing to 'round off' something, like we'll be doing when rounding the corners of our table mat, choose a saucer rather than a cup as your template because this curve will be much easier to sew.

1 Set up your sewing machine for use, as for the straight seam on page 24.

2 Sew around the curve slowly with the recommended seam allowance, gently pivoting the fabric with your non-dominant hand as you stitch and ensuring the presser foot hugs the edge of the fabric throughout.

TURNING THROUGH

This is just a fancy name for turning a project the nice way ('right side') out. The process of sewing two fabrics right sides together, then turning them right side out through a deliberate gap left in the seam, is also called 'bagging out'.

1

1 Unless stated otherwise you'll be sewing your projects together inside out ('right sides together'), and your pattern will have told you to leave a turning gap.

2 Simply remove the pins or clips then pull the right side of the project through the gap. Poke out the corners with the eraser end of a pencil to neaten these, then press the project to smooth.

2

Small gap?

If a turning gap seems small, most of the time you can still navigate the right side of the project through it – even bulky items, such as the bag on page 106, can crush down to fit through. If you are in any doubt though, snip a couple of stitches either side of the gap to make the gap slightly bigger – you don't want the fabric to tear.

ADDING LACE

This is much simpler than it sounds. You need only hold the lace in place temporarily with fabric glue, then secure it with stitching in a matching thread colour.

You can buy lace of different weights and styles from most hobby stores – for the one in our project, you'll want the heavier cotton kind.

1 Measure and cut the lace to fit the edge you're adding it to. Run a very fine line of glue (just enough to do the job) close to the edge of the mat, doing just a small section at a time. Once the glue is on, arrange the lace around the edge of the mat then press in place.

2 Allow the glued-on lace to dry completely (so you don't gum the machine needle with wet glue), then stitch over the top edge of the lace and the edge of the mat with zigzag stitch, using matching thread.

ADDING A LEATHER TAB

If you're looking to cover the ends of the lace, and add a professional finish to your item, you can stitch in a leather tab. Generally I like to cut a 2.5 x 6.5cm (1 x 2½in) strip, but the pattern will tell you exactly how big it needs to be.

While you could stitch the tab in place, a rivet will be much stronger and add a polished appearance to the project too. Always follow the manufacturer's instructions for your particular rivets.

1 To attach the tab, lightly glue it where it will go, straddling the frayed ends of the lace and wrapping it around the edge of the project.

2 Make a hole in the centre of the tab going through all layers.

3 Add a rivet to finish. Hardware can vary from brand to brand, so refer to the instructions that come with yours.

Table Mat with Lace

The epitome of 'cottage chic' is a table mat with a lace border that will show off your lovely pot of spring bulbs or a plate of freshly baked scones. To bring a modern edge to this vintage vibe, add a leather tab with a metal rivet – your grandmother would never have dreamt of such a thing!

SIZE

56 x 34cm (22 x 13½in)

SKILLS USED

- Using fusible interfacing (page 34)
- Rounding corners (page 34)
- Straight stitch (page 26)
- Sewing a seam (page 24)
- Sewing around a curve (page 35)
- Notching and clipping (page 25)
- Turning through (page 35)
- Top-stitch (page 27)
- Adding lace (page 36)
- Adding a leather tab (page 36)

PATTERN NOTES

All seam allowances are 5mm (¼in) unless otherwise stated.

When you are choosing your fabrics, I recommend the top print features a pretty floral pattern to ensure a cottage vibe.

YOU WILL NEED

Fabric:

- 56 x 45.75cm (22 x 18in) piece (or one Fat Quarter) of Fabric 1
- 56 x 45.75cm (22 x 18in) piece (or one Fat Quarter) of Fabric 2

Interfacing:

- 56 x 45.75cm (22 x 18in, or one Fat Quarter) of light-weight fusible fleece – I used H630 by Vlieseline®

Everything else:

- 163cm (64in) length of 2.5cm (1in) wide cotton lace
- 2.5 x 6.5cm (1 x 2½in) piece of leather or vegan leather
- Basic sewing tools (see page 8), plus a leather hole punch and rivet tools

TO CUT

From Fabric 1:

- One 54.5 x 37cm (21½ x 14½in) piece for the top fabric

From Fabric 2:

- One 54.5 x 37cm (21½ x 14½in) piece for the lining

From the interfacing:

- One 54.5 x 37cm (21½ x 14½in) piece

Instructions

1 Fuse the fleece to the WS of the fabric chosen for the top of the mat (Fabric 1).

2 Round the corners of the interfaced top panel. Repeat Steps 1 and 2 with the lining fabric (Fabric 2).

Creating curves

You do not need a fancy ruler to draw curves; tracing around an upturned saucer will do the trick.

3 Place the interfaced top panel RS together with the lining panel and pin or clip the edges.

4 Sew around the edge leaving a 10cm (4in) turning gap.

Where should I put my turning gap?

Leave the turning gap in the straightest (or one of the straightest) edges of your project; this makes it easier to close, as you don't have to navigate awkward angles.

5 Notch the four curved corners.

6 Turn out through the gap so the RS of the fabrics are facing out. Press the mat to make the edges sharp.

Closing a turning gap

There is no need to hand sew this turning gap closed. Fold the gap edges to the WS by 5mm (¼in) and press well. Lightly glue the edges and press to close. It will be sewn closed properly when we top-stitch in the next step.

7 Top-stitch around the edge 5mm (¼in) in from the edge.

8 Attach the lace: glue down first, leave to dry, then sew in place with zigzag stitch.

9 Wrap the leather tab around the edge of the mat, covering the raw ends of the lace, then glue. Make a hole in the tab through all the layers, then attach a rivet to finish.

Techniques

USING A TEMPLATE

Not every pattern has to have a template – particularly if, like the table mat on the previous pages, we're looking at just squares and rectangles that can be cut out easily with scissors (or a rotary cutter, ruler and cutting mat).

However, with shapes that are more complicated and can't be explained with a few measurements – like the darts in our upcoming trinket tray – a pattern template will make cutting out your project a breeze.

1 Trace the template given with the pattern instructions from the original source onto thin paper or tracing paper, then cut it out. Pin or clip the template onto the fabric – in this case, the corner.

2 Cut around the shape (or cut out the relevant pieces, like this 'V' shape on the corner) then remove the template.

MAKING DARTS

Darts are a great way to add shape and volume to a project. Or, as in the case of the upcoming trinket tray, to lift up fabric edges to create sides. Darts are typically triangular shaped; by bringing the edges of the triangle together then securing with stitches, it lifts the area of fabric to make it more 3D.

1 Using a template or following the instructions and measurements in the pattern, create the shape of the darts.

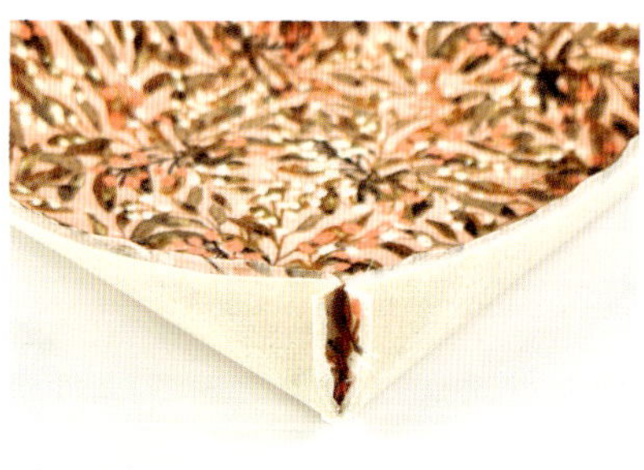

2 Pinch the sides of the dart right sides together and pin or clip in place. Sew along the length of the dart with a regular seam allowance (5mm / ¼in), backstitching at the beginning and end of the seam.

Easy Trinket Tray

It is simply astounding how useful these little trays are around the house! I use mine in my sewing room for buttons and threads, my art room for small tools and things that I need to reach for again and again, and all around the rest of the house for safe-keeping things like keys, coins and the usual everyday bits and bobs.

SIZE

24cm (9½in) square

SKILLS USED

- Using fusible interfacing (page 34)
- Using a template (page 42)
- Making darts (page 42)
- Straight stitch (page 26)
- Sewing a seam (page 24)
- Turning through (page 35)
- Edge-stitch (page 27)
- Top-stitch (page 27)

PATTERN NOTES

All seam allowances are 5mm (¼in) unless otherwise stated.

This tray can be easily resized up or down. Simply stick with a square and don't go much smaller than around 12.5cm (5in). The dart-corner template stays the same for all sizes.

YOU WILL NEED

Fabric:

- 25cm (10in) square OR one Fat Quarter (56 x 45.75cm / 22 x 18in) of Fabric 1
- 25cm (10in) square OR one Fat Quarter (56 x 45.75cm / 22 x 18in) of Fabric 2

Interfacing:

- 56 x 45.75cm (22 x 18in, or one Fat Quarter) of light-weight fusible fleece – I've used H630 by Vlieseline®
- 56 x 45.75cm (22 x 18in, or one Fat Quarter) of light-weight non-woven fusible interfacing – I've used Decovil I Light by Vlieseline®

Everything else:

- Basic sewing tools (see page 8)
- Dart-corner template on page 119

TO CUT

From Fabric 1 (if using a Fat Quarter):

- One 25cm (10in) square for the inside / top

From Fabric 2 (if using a Fat Quarter):

- One 25cm (10in) square for the outer / base

From the interfacing:

- One 25cm (10in) square from the light-weight fusible fleece
- One 25cm (10in) square from the very light-weight fusible interfacing

2
3
12
13
8
7
22
17
16
21
20
19
18
12.5"
12
12
17

Layering interfacing

If you need your interfacing to serve several functions in one project, the easiest thing to do is to layer up and secure multiple kinds of interfacing. In the case of this trinket tray, the fleece adds the softness I wanted, but the very light-weight interfacing gives the tray its much-needed stiffness to securely hold the valuables you'll put inside it.

1 Interface the WS of the inside / top panel of fabric with the fusible fleece. On top of this fusible fleece, fuse the slightly stiffer very light-weight interfacing. You should have three layers secured together.

2 Use the template on page 119 to mark and cut darts in all four corners of the interfaced top panel and the lining.

3 Sew the darts in the inside / top panel, RS sides together. Press the dart seams open as much as possible, as shown. Do the same for the outer / base panel.

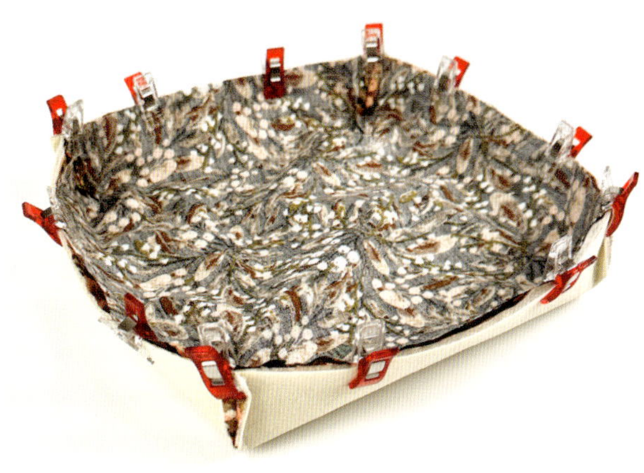

4 With RS together and the darts matched on the corners, pin or clip the lining to the top panel.

5 Sew around the top edge of the trinket tray, leaving an 8cm (3in) turning gap in one edge.

6 Turn the tray out through the turning gap, then turn the raw edges of the gap to the inside by 5mm (¼in). Press either side of the seamed edge so that it is perfect.

7 Edge-stitch around the top edge of the tray, about 3mm (⅛in) from the seam. This will close the turning gap at the same time, too.

8 Finish by sewing a second row of top-stitching, 5mm (¼in) below the first line.

Techniques

FEEDING IN ELASTIC

The good old-fashioned 'elastic in a fabric channel' method is a great way to pull in fabric and have it fit to an exact shape. It feels very old school, and indeed it is, but that doesn't mean that we should try to re-invent the wheel. This is a simple technique and very effective – they knew a thing or two, back in the day!

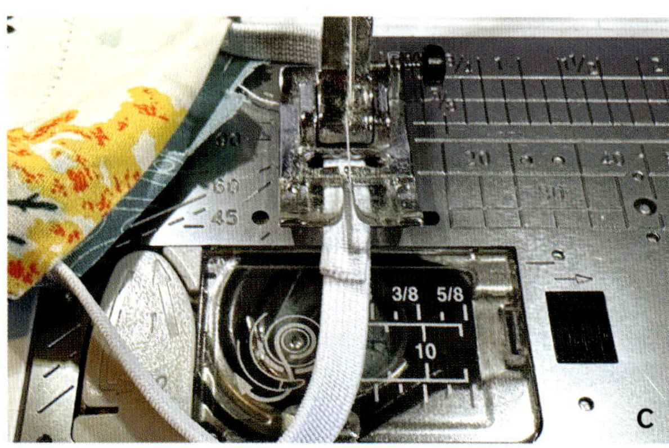

1 Measure and cut your elastic. To cut the appropriate length for your project, measure around the shape and then subtract 7.5cm (3in) from this number; this will be the length to cut.

2 Use something rigid to attach to the end of the elastic (**A**). I am using a 'proper' tool for this (Clip 'N' Glide Bodkin by Clover Mfg) but if you do not have one, pinning a regular safety pin to one end of the elastic will be perfect – just make sure that the safety pin is small enough to fit inside the channel you have made.

3 Feed the rigid tool into the gap left in the channel (**B**); it will pull the elastic with it.

4 With the help of your safety pin or tool, ease the elastic all the way round the inside of the channel until you are at the other side the gap. Bring the tool and the elastic out through the gap, remove the tool, then pin and sew the ends of the elastic securely together, overlapping the ends by about 2cm (¾in) (**C**).

5 Close the gap in the channel by hand with ladder stitch (**D**) – see page 29 for more on ladder stitch.

MAKING A CIRCULAR TEMPLATE

This pattern could simply have been written to fit one of the bowls in my kitchen – but there would not have been much point unless, by some random chance, you had bought exactly the same bowl! It's much easier to show you how to adapt the pattern to any size at all.

How much fabric do I need?

It has to be the diameter of your bowl (measure across the widest part) plus 5cm (2in) to allow for the sides. So if your bowl is 20cm (8in) in diameter, you will need a piece of fabric at least about 25cm (12½in) square.

1 Turn your chosen bowl upside down and centre it onto the wrong side of your desired fabric. Draw around the bowl with a fabric marker.

2 Use your ruler and fabric marker to measure and mark out a larger circle 5cm (2in) from the edge of the first circle with dots, moving the ruler as you work your way around. The closer your dots, the more accurate your circle in the next step will be.

3 Join the dots to make a larger circle.

4 Cut around the larger circle and use it as a pattern template for the lining.

Reversible Bowl Cover

I love finding yet another way to avoid using plastic in my kitchen. These bowl covers not only look lovely, but you can custom fit them to any bowl, and they are fully machine-washable too! If your cover is for a small bowl, you'll need very little fabric; so, you can use every bit of a beloved print. What's not to like?

SIZE

Varies, depending on your own bowl

SKILLS USED

- Making a circular template (page 49)
- Straight stitch (page 26)
- Sewing a seam (page 24)
- Sewing around a curve (page 35)
- Notching and clipping (page 25)
- Turning through (page 35)
- Top-stitch (page 27)
- Feeding in elastic (page 48)
- Ladder stitch (page 29)

PATTERN NOTES

All seam allowances are 5mm (¼in) unless otherwise stated.

All natural fabrics that are not too thick are suitable to use. Quilting cotton and linen are my favourites but you could also consider upcycling linens like old tablecloths or napkins.

YOU WILL NEED

Fabric:

- Two pieces of pretty fabric to fit your chosen bowl, one for the main fabric and one for the lining – the amount will depend on the size of your bowl

Everything else:

- Length of 5mm (¼in) wide woven elastic – to cut the appropriate length for your bowl, measure around the top of your bowl and then subtract 7.5cm (3in)
- Safety-pin, bodkin or Clip 'N' Glide Bodkin by Clover Mfg, to pull the elastic through the channel
- Basic sewing tools (see page 8)

TO CUT

From the fabrics:

- Cut one circle from each fabric, using the technique on page 49

Instructions

1 Pin or clip the main fabric and lining circles RS together. Sew almost all the way around the edge of the two layers with a 5mm (¼in) SA.

2 Notch the outer edge carefully; notching will help the shape sit neatly when turned through.

Raw edges of the gap

Fold the raw edges of the gap to the wrong side (i.e. the inside) of the cover by 5mm (¼in) then press well. This is so that the edges do not fray, and can be closed neatly in the final step.

3 Turn the right way out through the turning gap and press so that the edges are perfect.

4 Measure in 2.5cm (1in) all around and join the marks with your fabric marker to make a circle, as you did earlier.

5 Top-stitch along this line, then erase your marking appropriately (with an iron if it is a heat-erasable fabric marker, or water if it is a water-erasable fabric marker).

6 Attach one end of the elastic to your suitable tool or safety pin and feed it through the channel, making sure you don't twist the elastic.

7 Overlap the elastic ends by about 1.5cm (⅝in) and sew them together securely.

8 Sew the gap closed by hand with ladder stitch.

The reverse side of the bowl cover.

Techniques

USING SEW-IN INTERFACING

For some projects in this book, like the one coming up, you'll need a medium-weight interfacing with some squishiness to it. Wadding / batting (like 279 Cotton Mix 80/20 by Vlieseline®) is the kind of interfacing we're talking about here, and this type needs to be sewn in rather than fused into place with a hot iron.

While some patterns may ask you to cut the interfacing to the same size as the main fabric panel to which it's being attached (usually in dressmaking), in quilting you must cut the interfacing slightly larger than the main fabric panel to account for any shift in the fabric. The pillow cover on page 94 being an exception, you will also often have a backing panel to hide the interfacing on the wrong side of the project, and this will be larger than both the top (main) panel and the interfacing – for more on this see page 56.

To attach your interfacing, first lay your backing panel right side down and centre the interfacing on top of it. Your main fabric panel now goes centrally over the interfacing, its right side facing up. Pin in place going through all layers.

You cannot tack / baste around the edges of the fabric panel with a narrow seam allowance as you might in dressmaking, because it can cause the quilting layers to bunch up in the middle as you sew. For a project like ours, it must be secured with pins from the centre out to keep everything beautifully flat. You can buy special pins but most people use what they have. In home décor sewing, you will mainly use this sort of interfacing with these three layers.

QUILTING

Quilting is top-stitching's more glamorous cousin: it too involves stitching over the right side of the fabric for both a practical and decorative purpose, but the stitching tends to be more involved to create intricate-looking patterns. When quilting, you're securing three layers of material together – top fabric, wadding / batting and backing fabric – and at the same time creating an attractive design with your stitching. These three layers combined are commonly known as a 'quilt sandwich'.

For most quilting, it's important to fit your sewing machine with a walking (even- / dual-feed) foot beforehand (**A**); this foot acts like a second set of 'teeth' or feed dogs, and helps pull all the layers of material under the machine needle without distorting anything.

Use a slightly longer stitch length (around 3 to 3.5) than you use for regular sewing; these longer stitches accommodate the extra layers, and will stop the stitching pinching and puckering the fabric.

It's important to note that the top fabric in your quilt layers is usually about 2.5cm (1in) smaller all around than the wadding / batting and backing fabric (**B**); this is to compensate for any fabric creep (see the box, right).

Fabric creep

Fabric creep is not an official term (until now, that is!), but it is quite important when it comes to quilting. By 'fabric creep', I mean the natural movement of fabrics when being stitched. This movement is considerable when you are sewing through lots of layers (as you often do when quilting), and if this isn't counteracted in some way the whole project can get distorted while sewing. There are three ways to fix the problem: first, use a walking foot when sewing more than two layers; second, *always* cut the three layers of your 'quilt sandwich' so that the backing fabric and wadding / batting are larger than your top layer of fabric, known as the 'top fabric' (don't worry, the pattern will give details on sizes); and third, pin or clip your three layers securely before quilting.

A

B

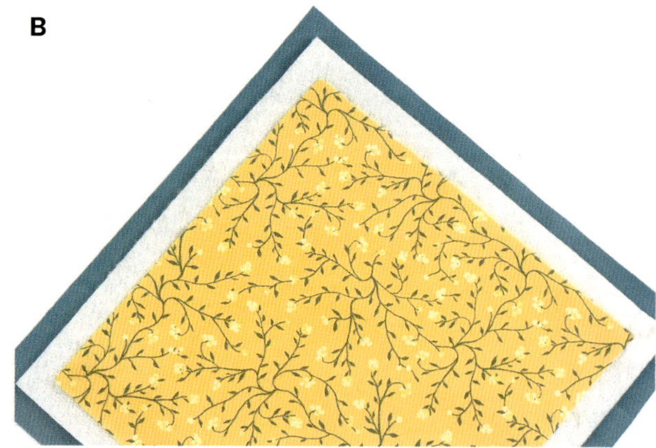

STRAIGHT-LINE QUILTING

This can be straight lines, straight-line grids, diagonal lines, or diagonal-line grids.

1 Decide on your quilting pattern then mark it on the top fabric with a fabric marker. In my case, I'm drawing a diagonal grid of lines. To begin with, I'm drawing my first set of lines at a 45-degree angle.

2 Once your lines are marked, sew over them: start from the wadding / batting (there's no need to reverse stitch), sew over the edge of the top fabric, then continue to stitch over your marked line. Finish the stitch line by sewing over the edge of the fabric on the other side, stitch a little way into the wadding / batting, then cut the thread. Again, there is no need to reverse stitch at the end of your stitch line. If your walking foot has a guide bar, as mine has, you need only draw your first two lines; then you can use the guide bar to help you accurately space your remaining lines (**C**).

3 Once my first set of lines were stitched, I measured, marked and quilted my second set of 45-degree lines, again only marking in the first two lines then using my walking foot's guide bar to help me space and sew the remaining quilt lines (**D**).

WAVY QUILTING

In essence, this is the same principle as straight-line quilting, but this time you do not need the guide bar. I think it's easier to wavy quilt than straight-line quilt as it's freeform and no-one can tell if 'mistakes' are part of the pattern or not...

Follow the process of quilting above (setting up the machine, ensuring your layers of material are prepared, your stitch length is correct, and stitching from and into the wadding / batting); however, instead of marking the fabric, simply twist the fabric left and right as you sew freehand to create 'waves' (**E**). They can be spaced at whatever distance you like, and the 'waves' don't need to look the same as each other either.

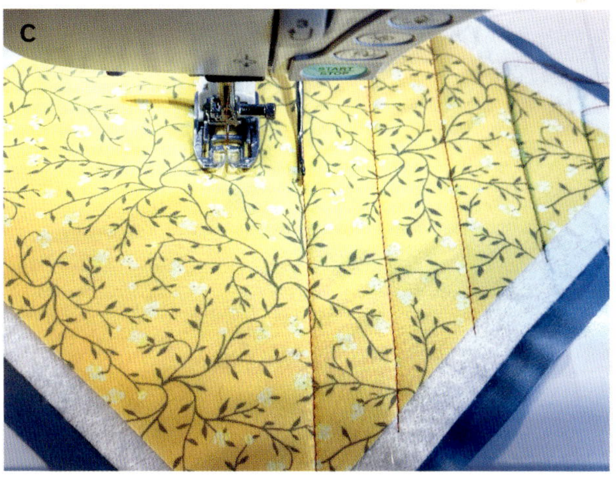

USING BINDING

WHAT IS BINDING?

There will sometimes be instances where you can't 'bag out' a project (see pages 20 and 35) and will need to sew the fabrics wrong sides together, leaving you with raw edges on the outside of the work. Most of the time, you'll want to cover these raw edges, not only for decorative purposes but also to prevent them from fraying and eventually coming apart. The most common way to cover the raw edges is to tuck them inside a long folded strip of fabric then sew this in place; this long strip is called 'binding'.

Depending on how the binding strips are cut, you can have 'straight binding' or 'bias binding'. Straight binding is made from a strip (or strips) of fabric cut along the straight grain of the fabric (either lengthwise or crosswise), and it's great for covering the edges of projects that are straight or right-angled. For projects that have curved edges, you'll want bias binding as this can neatly bend around curvy shapes with ease; this is thanks to the strip (or strips) for the binding being cut diagonally across the grain (or 'on the bias'), which gives the strip more stretch. If you need to familiarize yourself with fabric grain, turn back to page 14.

In this book, I've used only bias binding as I find this the most versatile of the two types since it can be used on both straight and curvy edges.

MAKING BIAS BINDING

Bias binding is readily available to buy in most craft stores and online, so you may be asking 'Why bother making your own?' The answer is that you have a world of fabric to choose from, but you're limited to a certain number of colours with ready-made bias binding, but if you make it yourself you can match it perfectly to your project. Making bias binding is also much easier than you think.

1 Cut bias strips of fabric as directed in the pattern. This means cutting on the diagonal, at a 45-degree angle to the straight grain.

2 To make one long, continuous strip, you'll need to join your bias strips together. To do this, first place the ends of the strips right sides together at right angles, the ends overreaching each other by 5mm (¼in) and leaving little 'ears'. Pin, then sew from one side of the uppermost binding to the other with a 5mm (¼in) seam allowance, as shown. When you open out the binding, you should have a straight strip joined on the bias.

3 Press the seam allowances open to reduce bulk. Continue to add strips until the required length is reached.

4 Fold the strip in half lengthways, wrong sides facing. Press, then open out the binding. Now, fold the longer edges towards the centre until they touch, wrong sides together, then press again. A bias tape maker is useful at this stage, as it does all the folding for you.

5 Re-fold the binding strips along the centre crease and press a final time. Roll the binding into a reel until it is needed, to store it neatly.

ATTACHING BIAS BINDING

You can attach binding by hand or by machine. I tend to use a combination both to ensure a nice neat finish – plus, a bit of hand sewing is a lovely way to relax in the evenings!

1 Trim the ends of the bias binding straight. Open out the binding then turn under one end by about 1cm (3/8in) and press.

2 Lay the opened-out binding along the edge of the project, right sides together and one long edge matching the raw edge of the fabric panel. Ensure the binding starts partway along a straight edge. Pin or clip in place.

3 Machine sew in place with the seam allowance detailed in the pattern. Depending on the width of your bias binding and the required seam allowance, in Step 3 you may be able to sew along the first crease line of the binding, and use this as a stitch-line guide.

4 The bias stretch in the tape will help you ease it around curved edges.

5 To join the ends of your binding neatly, once you've nearly finished stitching the binding to the front of the item, and when you reach the starting end of your binding, stop stitching. Lay the finishing end of your binding over the starting end (**5a**), allowing the raw edge of the finishing end to overlap the folded starting end by about 2.5cm (1in). You can trim any overhang beyond this amount (**5b**). Now stitch along the edge of the binding as before, stitching over the overlapped ends, until you've reached the beginning of the stitch line.

6 Now fold the free edge of the binding around the raw edges and over to the back of the project. No raw edges should be visible at this point, and the binding should cover the stitch line from sewing the binding to the front of the project. Pin or clip in place.

7 Hand sew this side of the binding to the back of the project with whip stitch (see page 28).

Double Oven Glove

Every kitchen needs a pot holder of some sort, and a double oven glove is doubly handy! This is a great project if you're beginning your quilting journey, as it covers all the basic techniques without needing to worry about sewing patchwork. This kind of quilting is called 'whole cloth quilting', which means quilting just one large piece of fabric, rather than a panel of multiple smaller pieces (which is patchwork).

SIZE

Approx. 20cm (8cm) wide x 67cm (26½in) long

SKILLS USED

- Using sew-in interfacing (page 54)
- Straight stitch (page 26)
- Quilting (page 56)
- Rounding corners (page 34)
- Sewing a seam (page 24)
- Sewing around a curve (page 35)
- Using binding (page 58)
- Whip stitch (page 28)

PATTERN NOTES

All seam allowances are 5mm (¼in) unless otherwise stated in the pattern.

This is a very simple quilt project and can be done on most home sewing machines. It is almost impossible to get 'wrong', and it is a great place to start your quilting journey.

The pot holder is made in three separate units (two are the glove pockets and the other is the long piece of fabric they're stitched to), then assembled and bound.

YOU WILL NEED

Fabric:

- 114 x 30cm (45 x 11¾in) square of Fabric 1, for the top fabric
- 114 x 50cm (45 x 19¾in) of Fabric 2, for the backing and binding fabric

Interfacing:

- 114 x 35cm (45 x 13¾in) of cotton-polyester mix medium-weight sew-in wadding / batting (such as 279 Cotton Mix 80/20 by Vlieseline®)

Everything else:

- Walking (even- / dual-feed) foot
- Basic sewing tools (see page 8)

TO CUT

From Fabric 1:

- One 68.5 x 20cm (27 x 8in) piece for the main panel top fabric
- Two 21.5 x 20cm (8½ x 8in) pieces, for the outer sides of the hand pockets – if your fabric is directional (i.e. the print 'points' in a particular direction), make sure the shorter edges of the fabric correspond with the top and bottom of the print

From Fabric 2:

- One 75 x 26cm (29½ x 10¼in) piece for the main panel backing fabric
- Two 27cm (10¾in) squares, for the inner / backing sides of the hand pockets
- Multiple 4cm (1½in) wide strips on the bias, joined to make a continuous length measuring at least 230cm (90½in) long

From the interfacing:

- One 74 x 25cm (29¼ x 10in) piece for the main panel interfacing
- Two 26 x 25cm (10¼ x 10in) pieces for the pocket interfacing

Instructions

1 Start making the quilt sandwich for the main panel: lay the backing for the main panel face (right side) down, centre the wadding / batting on top, then centre the main panel top fabric over the two layers, as shown. Pin (don't clip) in place. Repeat with the pocket pieces, keeping them separate from the main panel for now.

2 Set up your machine up for quilting, including installing your walking foot and adjusting the stitch length. Referring to the information on pages 56 and 57, quilt over the layers of the main panel and pockets with your chosen quilting design, remembering to stitch from and into the wadding / batting. To keep things simple, I recommend using a diagonal wave design.

3 For both the main panel and the pockets, trim the layers back to the size of the top pieces.

4 Round the four corners of the main panel – to do this, grab a small plate or mug, turn it upside down, lay this over each corner and trace around it with a fabric pen, then cut along your markings.

5 Repeat with the pocket pieces, this time at two corners of each piece only. If your fabric is directional (i.e. the print 'points' in a particular direction), make sure the rounded corners will sit at the bottom of the print.

Directional fabric

If you've used directional fabric, in the next few stages you'll see why it was important to round the correct corners of the pocket pieces: by rounding the corners at the 'bottom' of the print, it means the bottom of the pockets nicely align with the ends of the main glove panel.

6 From the continuous length of binding, cut two 21cm (8¼in) lengths. Bind the straight edges of the pocket pieces with these lengths of bias binding. Cut away any overhang.

7 Pin or clip the pockets onto the main panel, aligning the edges and rounded corners. Machine tack / baste the outer edges of the pockets to the main glove panel, stitching $\frac{1}{8}$in (3mm) from the raw edges – this is called 'stitching within the seam allowance'. By doing this you avoid sewing on top of previous stitching, and adding bulk into the seam.

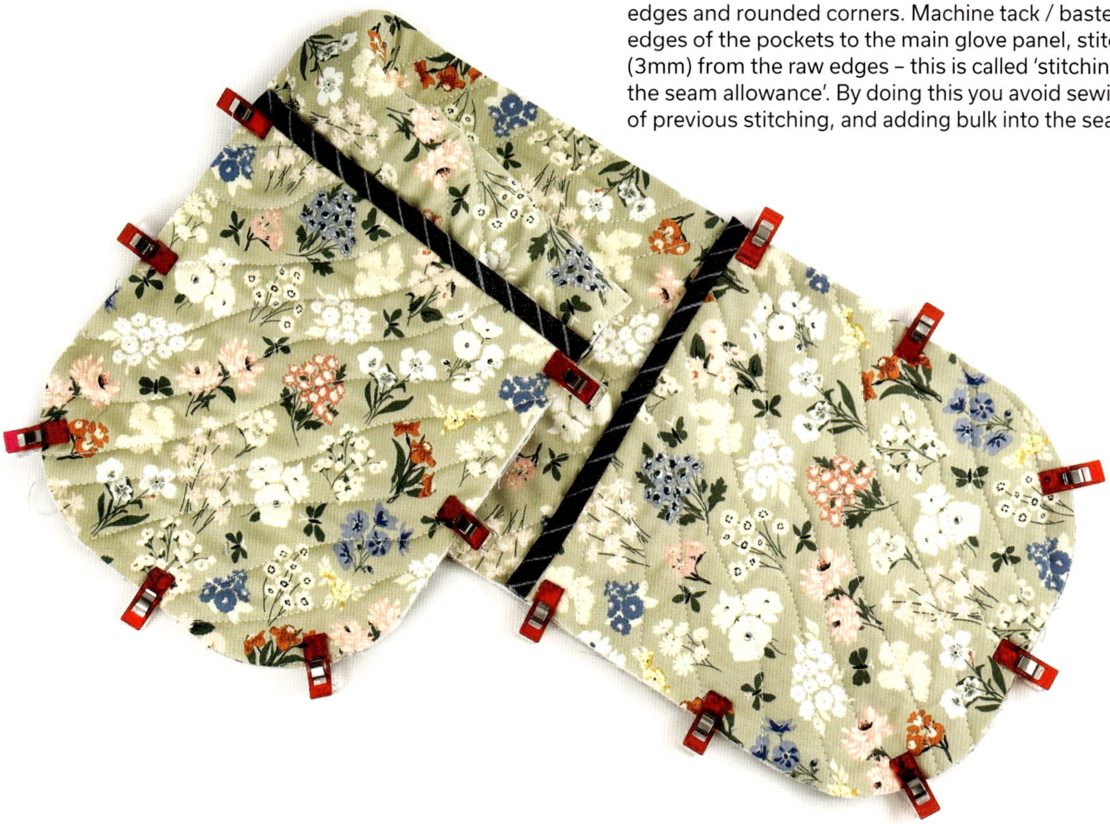

8 Attach the rest of the binding to the outer edge of the whole glove panel, machine sewing from the top of the fabric for the first side of the binding...

... and hand-sewing the other side of the binding to the back of the gloves with whip stitch.

Techniques

ADDING METAL PRESS SNAP FASTENERS

Nothing, I repeat, *nothing* raises the status of your masterpiece like adding metal hardware! I highlighted this earlier on, but always purchase the best materials that you can afford; if you choose wisely, some packs will even come with the fitting tools required to secure them in place.

To fit each metal snap fastening, you'll need all the components that make up the fastening (typically these are the cap, socket, stud and post), and the fitting tools recommended for your particular brand.

There are many brands of hardware available, each with slightly different fitting instructions, so I've kept the information here general. I tend to stick with Prym, and that is the brand that I will be using. Some brands will have a little hole punch as part of their fitting kits, but I prefer to use an old-fashioned leather punch.

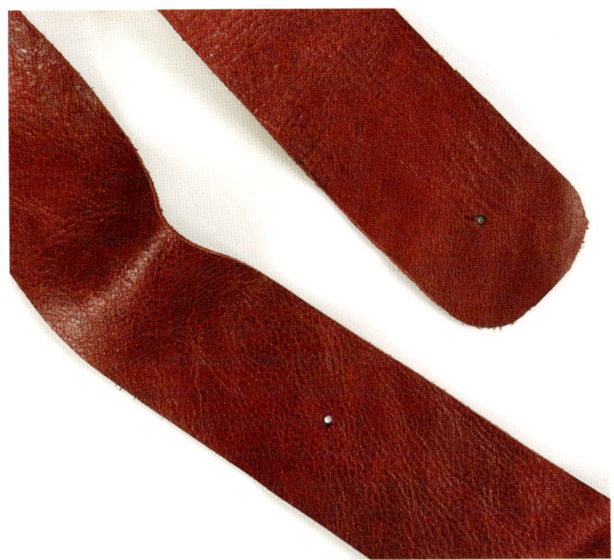

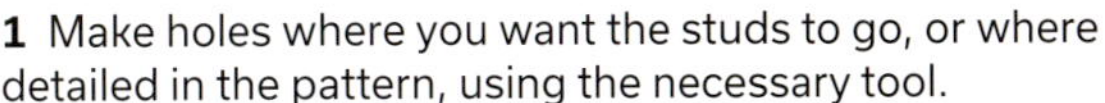

1 Make holes where you want the studs to go, or where detailed in the pattern, using the necessary tool.

2 The 'male' half and the 'female' half of the fastening will each have two parts. Sometimes these will be brand specific, so refer to the information on the packet, but generally the female half will consist of the cap and socket, and the male half the stud and post.

Check twice, fit once

Before you commit to fitting the fastening, double-check the holes are in the right place and that the parts of the fastening will be facing the right way at the end. Usually, the cap and stud will be facing outwards; the socket and post will be facing the inside of the project.

3 Attach the male half as detailed in the packet instructions, using the necessary fitting tools. The right side of the stud will be on the right side of the strap.

4 Attach the female half of the stud to finish.

MEASURING AND MAKING A SIMPLE CASE TEMPLATE

Most of the time we can find a great pattern that fits our needs exactly. However, now and then it is just not possible – or required.

The laptop sleeve on the next page is a great example. It is just a simple rectangle that is then folded and sewn. It fits my laptop exactly, but what if yours is a different size? Here's how to measure your own device and make a template from it.

1 Measure your device across the widest part. You'll then need to add two more figures to this: add 2.5cm (1in) for 'ease' (this means adding a little 'breathing room' for the item you're covering so it can move inside the case) and then add 1cm (½in) for the seam allowance (as you're adding 5mm / ¼in to both the left- and right-hand edges).

2 Now measure your laptop vertically, again adding 2.5cm (1in) to the figure for ease. There is no need for a seam allowance this time. Double this figure to cover both the front and back of your device.

3 Finally, the flap. The flap is actually an extension of the case front/back, and needs to be about half the height of the device. Simply halve the vertical measurement taken in Step 2, then add it to your vertical measurement.

4 Before cutting out your fabric, I recommend drawing your template onto paper first – you could use 'proper' pattern drafting paper for this, or simply tape multiple sheets of copy paper together. For my template, I've drawn a rectangle that is 35cm (13¾in) wide (device width + ease + seam allowance) and 60cm (23½in) long (front of device + back of device + ease + flap). Cut out your paper pattern then wrap this around your device to check the size. If it is too big or too small, double-check your measurements. If it is about perfect, you're ready to cut out your fabric.

Felt Laptop Sleeve

Give your precious laptop an easy-to-sew protective sleeve. Specific dimensions are not given in this pattern, so you can custom fit the sleeve to your own laptop. This sleeve pattern could also be adapted to other slimline devices such as a tablet, an e-reader or a digital notepad.

SIZE

Varies, depending on your own device

SKILLS USED

- Measuring and making a simple case template (page 70)
- Using fusible interfacing (page 34)
- Rounding corners (page 34)
- Straight stitch (page 26)
- Sewing a seam (page 24)
- Sewing around a curve (page 35)
- Adding metal press snap fasteners (page 68)
- Top-stitch (page 27)

handmade
"FOR EVERY
CREATED
A MOOD BOARD... AND THEN
I'D SLOWLY WORK FROM THAT"

PATTERN NOTES

All seam allowances are 5mm (¼in) unless otherwise stated in the pattern.

You may be familiar with felt squares made for crafting, but we're looking for pure wool felt off the bolt. This is because we need this to be quite long to wrap around the laptop.

For the strap, look for thin clothing-weight leather that won't tax your machine too much. Otherwise opt for vegan leather, cork or even a piece of felt that's in a contrast colour.

Double-sided tape is brilliant for holding the strap pieces in place before sewing.

YOU WILL NEED

Fabric:

- Final width and vertical measurements (see pages 70 and 71) of felt in colour 1, for the sleeve outer
- Final width and vertical measurements (see pages 70 and 71) of felt in colour 2, for the sleeve lining
- 5cm (2in) wide strip of thin leather, vegan leather, cork or alternative, for the strap – calculate the length required by adding 8cm (3in) to the length of the outer felt piece

Interfacing:

- Final width and vertical measurements (see pages 70 and 71) of Iron-on, paper-backed adhesive web – I used Bondaweb by Vlieseline®

Everything else:

- One metal press fastening and the hardware to fit it (if you're using the older method like I am, you'll also need a mallet or hammer) – my set is a 15mm (⅝in) diameter press fastener by Prym
- Double-sided tape, for holding the strap in place in Steps 9 and 10
- Basic sewing tools (see page 8)
- Optional: walking (even- / dual-feed) foot, if you're sewing with leather, vegan leather or cork

Instructions

1 Position the piece of adhesive web centrally over one piece of felt, the paper side facing up. Fuse in place with an iron, referring to the instructions on the packet.

2 Remove the paper backing on the adhesive web. Centre the other piece of felt over the top then fuse in place with an iron. Both felt pieces should now be stuck together.

3 Round two corners on one short side of your felt rectangle, using a mug or small plate as a template to draw and then cut around; this will form the flap.

4 Round the two corners at one end of the strap piece. Measure and mark 2.5cm (1in) in from this end, centrally, then make a hole. At the other (square) end of the strap, measure and mark 17cm (6¾in) in from the end, centrally, and make another hole.

5 Double-check the holes are in the correct place by wrapping the strap around the folded felt (folded to account for the front, back and flap sections) then marking a dot through the hole in the rounded end with a fabric marker.

6 Attach the male half of the press fastening in the hole at the square end of the strap, using the necessary fitting tools and making sure the stud piece is on the outer side (RS) of the strap.

7 Attach the female half of the press fastening in the hole at the rounded end of the strap, using the necessary fitting tools and making sure the cap piece is on the outer (RS) side of the strap.

8 Flip the felt panel so the outer side is facing up. Find the vertical centre on the felt panel and mark it with a line. The simplest way to do this is to fold the panel in half, long edges together, finger-press to crease, then unfold.

9 Lay the strap centrally over the marked line, making sure its RS is facing up, its straight end is flush with the straight edge of the felt panel, and the rounded end overlaps the rounded edge of the felt panel, as shown. Secure in place by sticking a piece of double-sided tape to the WS of the strap, then positioning the strap on the felt panel.

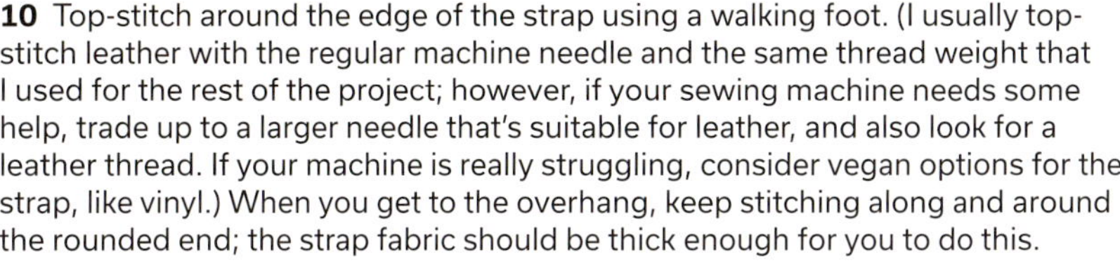

10 Top-stitch around the edge of the strap using a walking foot. (I usually top-stitch leather with the regular machine needle and the same thread weight that I used for the rest of the project; however, if your sewing machine needs some help, trade up to a larger needle that's suitable for leather, and also look for a leather thread. If your machine is really struggling, consider vegan options for the strap, like vinyl.) When you get to the overhang, keep stitching along and around the rounded end; the strap fabric should be thick enough for you to do this.

11 Fold the short, straight edge of the sleeve up to the base of the flap section, as shown. Check that your device fits in and mark its position. Unfold the felt, then top-stitch along the short, straight edge only.

12 Fold the felt panel again, up to the marked position. Pin the sides in place. Starting from the bottom corner of one side of the sleeve, top-stitch up the side, around the opened flap and down the other side to finish.

Techniques

WHAT IS APPLIQUÉ?

Appliqué is a decorative sewing technique that involves stitching fabric shapes onto a larger background fabric to create a motif or pattern. The shapes you use depend on the picture or pattern you're creating.

If you're looking to add more elaborate designs to your sewing projects, without using methods like embroidery, appliqué is a great way to do this. It's often used in quiltmaking, either by itself or together with patchwork techniques, to create intricate quilt tops – mainly what are called 'pictorial quilts', which are quilts that feature scenes or detailed subjects.

There are several different kinds of appliqué, and some are worked entirely by hand or machine. For this book, we're focusing on machine appliqué.

RAGGY EDGE APPLIQUÉ

Raggy edge appliqué is one of the easiest forms of machine appliqué, as you don't need to neaten the edges of the fabric shapes. All you do is cut the necessary appliqué shapes from your fabric, position them on your background fabric, then just stitch around the edge of the shape with a regular straight stitch and a narrow seam allowance.

The stitching around each shape stops the fabric from fraying *too* much, but otherwise (as the name suggests) you deliberately allow the edges to fray a bit to create a beautifully relaxed form of appliqué that looks artistic and textured.

To stop your shapes from moving around while you are stitching them, you can use a fabric glue or a special heat-bondable interfacing. I usually opt for the second and that is what I have used in this project.

To ensure you can stitch around your shapes with lots of freedom, and without fighting with your sewing machine's nature to pull the fabric under the foot in one direction, you will need to set the stitch length to '0'. When you do this, you'll find you can move the fabric almost limitlessly, and it means that you can pretty much 'draw' with your sewing machine. This type of sewing and set-up is called 'free-motion embroidery' – more on this in the tip box on page 80.

Darning foot for free-motion embroidery (see the tip box on page 80)

1 If you're using iron-on, paper-backed adhesive web (such as Bondaweb by Vlieseline®) like me, first draw your shapes onto the paper side of the web. Cut them out roughly, leaving a little 'border' around each shape to trim back later.

2 Fuse the pieces onto the wrong side of the relevant fabrics, then cut out the shapes exactly.

3 'Build' your design with the shapes, over the background fabric. If your design is from a pattern, and there are certain shapes sitting behind other shapes, the instructions or templates will tell you this. When you're happy with the arrangement, tear away the paper backing, then fuse each shape to the background fabric in turn, starting with the 'bottom' pieces that sit under all the other shapes then working your way forwards.

4 If you're new to free-motion embroidery, I recommend drawing the details onto your shape to start with using your fabric marker; this way, you have guidelines to follow with your needle.

5 Set up your machine for free-motion embroidery (see the tip box, right). Using a 3mm (⅛in) 'seam allowance', stitch around the shapes and add details, referring to the instructions, template and your own drawn guidelines. When you move to stitch the next shape, simply raise the needle, move the design under the foot until you're above the next shape, then lower the needle – there's no need to cut the thread.

6 Once your design is completely stitched, snip the linking threads close to the fabric; don't worry, the threads shouldn't unravel.

Free-motion embroidery

To set up your machine for free-motion embroidery, you'll need to do the following:

- Set the stitch length to '0'.
- Change the universal presser foot to a darning / free-motion foot. If you haven't invested in one of these yet, and you have a basic sewing machine model, you can sew without a foot in place and just with the needle, *but* you'll need to be extremely careful when sewing to ensure you don't stitch over your fingers by accident!
- Optional: drop the feed dogs (see the photograph above) – these are the little 'toothy bits' poking up through the needle plate, and their job is to feed the fabric under the foot in regular sewing to make the stitches even. If you have an older or basic sewing machine, you may not be able to lower the feed dogs – don't panic; setting the stitch length to '0' should compensate for the slight pull.

USING FOAM INTERFACING

Foam interfacing is great for adding depth and structure to a project, plus it's washable too. I like to use sew-in rather than fusible foam interfacing, as it's easier to attach when you have several layers of fabric to handle; there's also less risk of squashing all the lovely detail in your project with the iron!

1 Cut the foam a little bit larger all around than the panel you're interfacing – roughly 2cm (¾in) on all edges is about right. Centre your panel over the foam, its right side facing up. Pin in place.

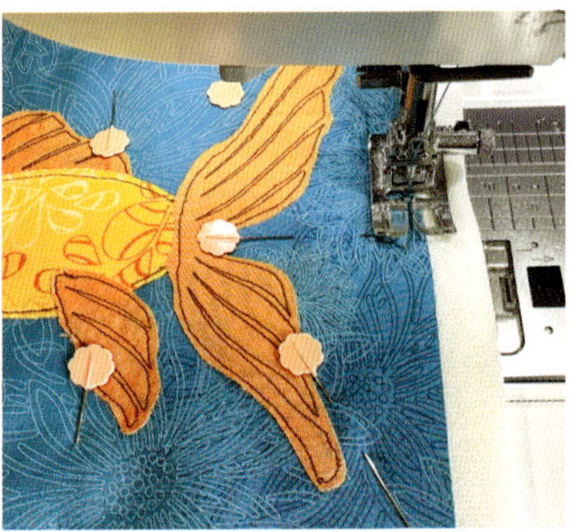

2 You now need to secure the foam to the fabric panel with stitches – these need to be longer than usual to account for the bulk. Change the stitch length on your machine to 4 or 5 (to make the stitches longer). Using a narrow seam allowance of 3mm (⅛in), sew all around the edge of the fabric panel as shown.

3 Trim the foam interfacing back to the edge of the exterior panel. The panel is ready to use.

Sewing within the seam allowance

If a specific seam allowance is dictated in your pattern (usually this is 5mm / ¼in), but you're then asked to stitch close to the edge of the fabric, it's likely you're being asked to 'sew within the seam allowance'.

By stitching within the seam allowance, it means you won't be sewing over this stitching later on, when sewing your particular panel of fabric to another fabric panel.

Sewing over an existing seam is problematic: it'll create too much bulk in the seam, and there's a big risk of your needle getting stuck in the stitching and pulling the work into the sewing machine.

MAKING SQUARE CORNERS

Squaring corners is a sewing technique that ensures your sewing project transforms into a 3D shape with sharp corners.

There are a few ways to do this. It can be as simple as cutting off the corners at a diagonal angle – making sure not to snip into the stitching – once two fabric panels have been stitched right sides together. But for bulky projects like the one coming up, we have to take a slightly different approach.

If you've interfaced your project with thick interfacing like foam interfacing, its bulkiness will make it difficult to achieve sharp corners when the seams are stitched in the usual way – if we simply sew from raw edge to raw edge, the corners will be rounded. The remedy is to stitch short of each corner. Let's look at this in more detail...

1 On the wrong sides of your fabric panels (i.e. the side with the interfacing), from each corner measure in by 5mm (¼in) and make a clear mark with a fabric marker.

2 Pin or clip the pieces to be sewn right sides together. Set up your machine with a walking (even- / dual-feed) foot; this will help you stitch through the bulkiness. Sew the seam, starting and stopping at the marks and reverse stitching at each end. Repeat to add the remaining necessary panels.

3 Once all the panels are stitched together, turn through the project so that right side is facing out. Using the eraser end of a pencil, gently push the corners out so that they are as sharp as possible.

1

2

3

3D LINING

Lining your makes elevates them straight away. We have already lined several things but this lining is a little different in that we're making it into a 3D shape. Don't worry, it's easy!

1 Sew the lining pieces together in the same way you stitched the outer panels (if you've used bulky interfacing, you'll need to sew the lining panels as detailed opposite, to make the corners nice and square); however, in the middle of one seam, leave a small turning gap. This gap needs to be large enough to turn the whole outer through, so don't make it too small – a gap of approximately 8cm (3in) is about right. And there's no need to reverse stitch at either side of the turning gap; if your stitches come undone at either side of the gap, you can just re-stitch them later.

2 If you haven't already, turn through the project outer so its right side is facing out. Keep the lining inside out. Pull the lining over the exterior, so that the right sides are together. The lining will be quite a snug fit, but this ensures it's smooth when it is turned the right way out.

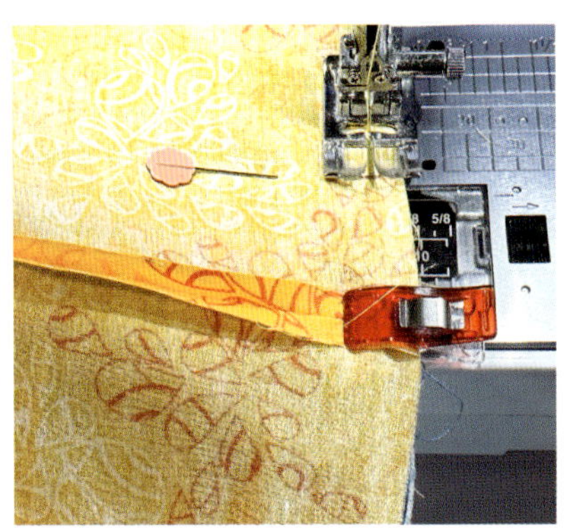

3 Carefully line up the corners and the top edges, then pin or clip in place. Sew right around the top edge of the project with the seam allowance detailed in the pattern, leaving no gaps.

4 Turn out through the gap in the base and close the turning gap by hand or by machine.

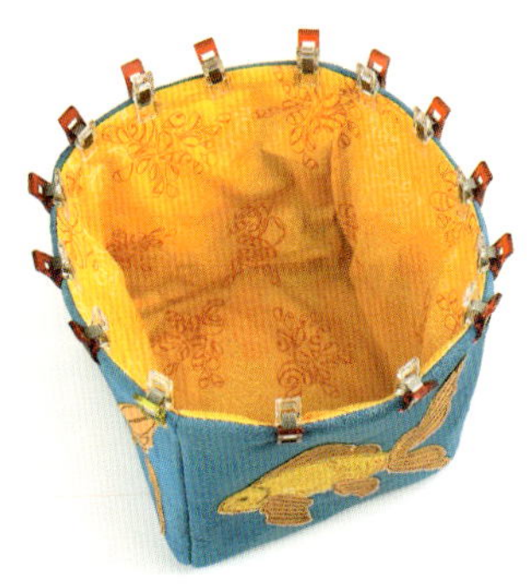

5 Stuff the lining down into the outer shape, and adjust so that the top seam lies perfectly along the top edge. Pin or clip in place before top-stitching all around the top edge from the outer side with coordinating thread.

Appliqué Storage Cube

We all need more storage in our lives and the prettier it is, the better! This little cube is very much at home in a bathroom or baby's room, and it is something you will want to make again and again.

SIZE

15cm (6in) square

SKILLS USED

- Using fusible interfacing (page 34)
- Raggy edge appliqué (page 78)
- Using foam interfacing (page 81)
- Edge-stitch (page 27)
- Sewing a seam (page 24)
- Straight stitch (page 26)
- Making square corners (page 82)
- 3D lining (page 83)
- Turning through (page 35)
- Ladder stitch (page 29)
- Top-stitch (page 27)

PATTERN NOTES

All seam allowances are 5mm (¼in) unless otherwise stated.

You will need templates for the appliqué (provided on page 119). The dashed lines on a template indicate where it sits behind another template.

Use your fabric marker to add in as many details as you need to when preparing the appliqué. These can be removed later on.

YOU WILL NEED

Fabric:

- 114 x 23cm (45 x 9in) of Fabric 1, for the outer panels – mine is a blue shade
- 114 x 46cm (45 x 18¼in) of Fabric 2, for the lining panels and the goldfish body – I used a gold-yellow fabric colour
- Fat Eighth (56 x 23cm / 23 x 9in) of Fabric 3, for the goldfish fins and goldfish tail – mine is an orange shade

Interfacing:

- 50 x 45.75cm (20 x 18in) of iron-on paper-backed adhesive web (such as Bondaweb by Vlieseline®), for the appliqué
- 114 x 18cm (45 x 7in) strip of medium-weight fusible cotton interlining (such as G740 by Vlieseline®), for interfacing the outer panels
- 114 x 45.75cm (45 x 18in) of light-weight sew-in foam interfacing (such as Style-Vil by Vlieseline®), for the extra interfacing on the outer panels

Everything else:

- Matching thread for the appliqué – I used a golden brown shade
- Templates on page 119
- Basic sewing tools (see page 8)
- Optional: darning / free-motion foot

TO CUT

From Fabric 1:

- Five 16.5cm (6½in) squares for the outer panels

From Fabric 2:

- Five 15cm (6in) squares for the lining panels
- Four fish bodies using the template on page 119

From Fabric 3:

- Five 15cm (6in) squares for the lining panels
- Four fish bodies using the template on page 119

Interfacing:

- Five 16.5cm (6½in) squares of medium-weight fusible cotton interlining, for interfacing the outer panels
- Five 21cm (8¼in) squares of light-weight sew-in foam interfacing, for the extra interfacing on the outer panels

Fat Eighth

This is another available pre-cut that is slightly less popular than the Fat Quarter. You might have guessed this is half the size of a Fat Quarter; however, depending on how you cut a Fat Quarter, a Fat Eighth can be a 'slim' cut (56 x 23cm / 22 x 9in) or a 'fat' cut (28 x 45.75cm / 11 x 18in). The 'slim' cut is the most commonly used and available, and is what I've used in this pattern.

Instructions

1 Fuse each square of cotton interlining to the WS of a Fabric 1 square. Set aside one of the squares; this will be the base of the cube.

2 The adhesive web has a rough (glue) and a smooth (paper) side. Trace the goldfish pieces onto the smooth paper side and cut the shapes out roughly. You need enough shapes to make four goldfish in total. Fuse the glue side of the pieces onto the WS of the relevant fabrics (Fabric 2 for bodies; Fabric 3 for the fins and tails) then cut them out exactly, as shown.

3 Without securing anything in place, build the goldfish motif centrally over the RS of each interfaced Fabric 1 square, referring to the positioning on the original template. Note that the appliqué pieces with a dashed line indicate they sit underneath another appliqué shape. When you're happy with the arrangement, fuse the shapes in place, working from the back pieces to the front pieces: top fin, body, then lower fins and tail.

4 If you wish, draw the goldfish details on to the appliqué shapes with a fabric marker to use as guidelines. Set up your machine for free-motion embroidery, then stitch the goldfish details onto each square.

5 Lay each Fabric 1 square, including the set-aside base piece, centrally over a square of foam interfacing then pin in place. Set up your machine with a walking foot, then stitch all around the edges of each Fabric 1 square with a 3mm (1⁄8in) SA (i.e. within the main SA), using a longer stitch length. Trim the foam interfacing back to the size of the Fabric 1 square, after the foam has been stitched in place.

6 Make sure your walking foot is installed in your sewing machine, as it's going to get bulky! Pin or clip then sew the Fabric 1 outer goldfish squares RS together side by side in a row, stopping and starting 5mm (1⁄4in) from each corner to avoid bulk in the seams. In the same way, pin or clip then sew the sides of the far-left and far-right goldfish squares RS together to join them into a square. Finally, clip and sew in the base.

Sewing in the base

The base will be tricky to stitch because of the bulkiness, but just take it slowly and don't try to pull the fabric through manually to speed up the process – you'll find the walking foot and feed dogs should do their job.

If your machine has the option, remove the accessory compartment to access the free arm; this will allow you to slide the cube over the arm, and make the stitching process a little easier and more comfortable.

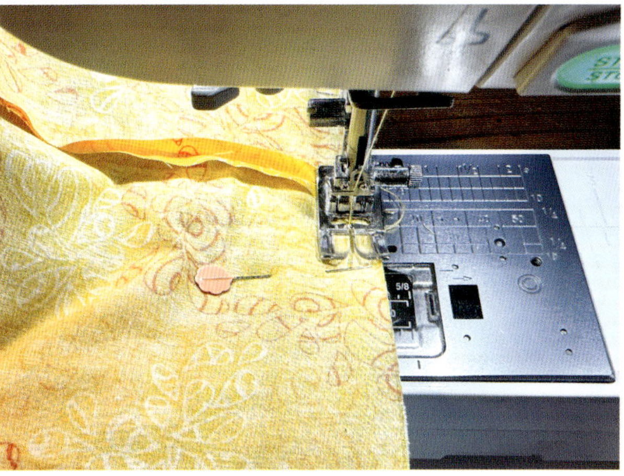

7 Sew the Fabric 2 lining squares together in the same way as the Fabric 1 outer squares, this time leaving an 8cm (3in) gap in one seam. Turn the Fabric 1 outer cube RS out, poking out the corners with the blunt end of a pencil to make them nice and sharp. Leave the Fabric 2 lining cube inside out. Pull the lining cube over the outer cube, RS facing, then pin and/or clip in place, matching the seams and top edges.

8 Sew right around the top edge of both the outer and lining cubes, leaving no gaps.

9 Turn the whole project out through the gap in the lining cube.

10 Hand-sew the gap closed in the lining using ladder stitch.

11 Push the lining down into the cube and make sure that the top edge is perfect. Top-stitch around the top edge of the cube, stitching from the RS, to secure the lining and finish the project.

Techniques

FINISHING SEAMS WITH ZIGZAG STITCH

Up until this point we've not really needed to finish our seams, as projects have been either suitably lined – squished between other layers – or we've not used the kind of fabric that requires it. However, for our next project, we'll need to finish the seams.

What does 'finishing a seam' mean? Basically, it means securing the raw edge of the seam, often with an decorative stitch. I have chosen zigzag stitch because pretty much every machine has this option, but you can also use any other decorative stitches that your sewing machine offers, or even an overlocker (serger) if you have one (see the tip, right).

Finishing a seam adds a lovely professional finish to your project, and it stops fabrics that are prone to fraying (I'm looking at you, cotton and linen!) from coming apart with time and wear.

The simplest way to finish a seam is to use a zigzag stitch. All you need to do is switch the stitch type on your sewing machine to a wide enough zigzag stitch (wide enough to cover your seam allowance), align the presser foot so that the zigzag will sew slightly over the raw edge of the fabric, then stitch as you would sew a seam – the zigzag should 'bind' the edge of your fabric.

Using an overlocker/serger

You may be familiar with an overlocker (or serger) – this is a special sewing machine that creates a highly professional finished edge on sewing projects, as it simultaneously trims the fabric neatly and sews a finishing stitch (called an overlock / serge stitch).

An overlocker is used mainly by dressmakers, especially if they're sewing with stretchy fabrics like jersey. And if you get super serious with your sewing, an overlocker is a useful investment.

However, as a beginner sewist it's not necessary to buy an overlocker. In fact, I have been sewing for over 40 years and I still don't own one! A sewing machine's zigzag stitch does the job just as nicely.

If you're keen to experiment, some sewing machine models come with an overcast stitch that creates a similar appearance to overlock / serge stitch; you may need to purchase a special foot, called an 'overlock foot', to sew successfully with this stitch.

ADDING A ZIP

For some reason, adding zips sends cold chills down the spines of new sewists. I think that it is something to do with the limitations of older machines back in the day, and the horror stories about battling with different sewing notions to compensate for the one presser foot. Those days are happily behind us, and we can confidently sew zips in the knowledge that we have better tools at our disposal.

You will need your zipper foot for this, as it has special indents close to the needle that allow you to stitch close to zip teeth. The rest of the sewing process is pretty much the same as regular sewing.

Zipper foot

A

B

C

D

1 For basic zip attachment, you'll be sewing a zip between two panels of fabric. Take your first panel of fabric and lay it right side up. Lay the zip face down along the edge of the appropriate panel, the zip facing down and matching one of its edges to the raw edge of the panel. Clip or pin the zip in place (**A**).

2 Swap out your regular sewing foot for a zipper foot, referring to your sewing machine manual. Using the seam allowance detailed in the pattern, stitch along the edge of the zip (**B**) – you'll notice you can stitch relatively close to the zip teeth.

3 Fold the zip back, so that its right side is facing up, then top-stitch along the edge of the zip; this helps to push the fabric down (**C**).

4 Repeat the process on the other side of the zip with the second fabric panel (**D**).

MAKING PIPING

Piping is a kind of decorative edging comprising a length of cord stitched inside bias tape. Sewing piping to the edge of a project gives it a lovely rounded, 3D border.

To make piping, you will need a zipper foot, a long length of piping cord that's 5–6mm (¼in) thick, and some bias tape. You can buy bias tape for this purpose, or make your own as outlined on page 59. In addition, I find some fabric glue is really handy when making the piping.

1 Trim the ends of the piping cord to remove any frayed sections. Lay the cord over the wrong side of your hand-made or purchased bias tape.

2 Run some glue along the bias tape, just on one side of the piping cord.

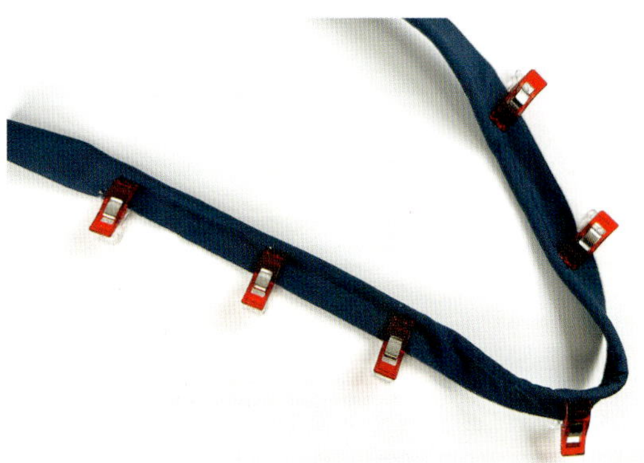

3 Close the tape over the cord and press down onto the line of glue. Pin or clip, then allow to dry completely (else the glue will gum the sewing machine needle later). The glue will keep the bias tape in place around the piping cord while you sew, without needing pins.

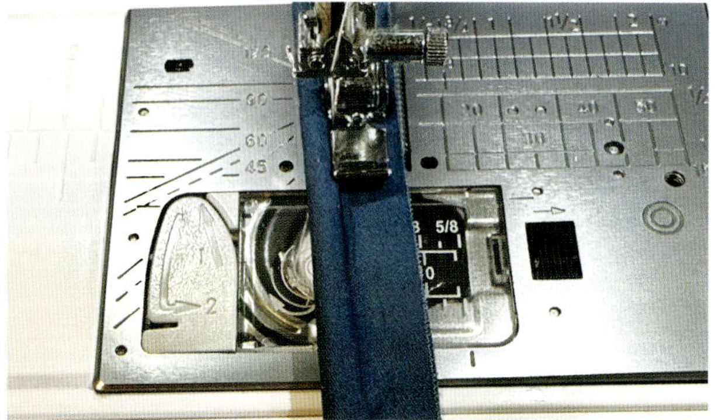

4 Install the zipper foot on your sewing machine (see also the tip below). Sew along the length of the piping, stitching very close to the cord.

Using a zipper foot for piping

The zipper foot allows you to get in super-close to the cord, so you can make a strong, rigid length of piping with no floppiness.

ADDING A TASSEL

This is technically not a sewing technique, but making tassels is a great skill to know for most craft projects. Tassels are very easy to make, and are lovely textured, decorative additions to things like zipper pulls. I've got a method that uses several skeins of stranded embroidery thread / floss at once, for a quick and easy tassel.

1 Carefully pull out and cut a length of thread / floss from one of the skeins that's about 35cm (13¾in) long. Make sure that you do not upset the shape of the skein – leaving the paper wrappings on helps with this.

2 Divide the cut length into two bundles, with three strands in each bundle.

3 Place two skeins next to each other. Use one bundle of strands from Step 2 to tie the two skeins together securely at the centre.

4 Fold the two skeins together. Wrap the remaining bundle of strands around the skeins, about 1.5cm (¾in) down from the fold.

5 Remove the paper sleeves and trim the bottom of the tassel level to make the ends neat.

6 Thread the top tie onto a needle with a large eye. Use this to secure the tassel to your project, then trim away the excess.

Quilted & Zipped Pillow Cover

Sewing your own pillow covers is not only easy but a great way to ensure you have *the* fabric that works perfectly with your existing décor. To take your sewing skills to the next level, and elevate your pillow cover design, we'll add some quilting for extra texture, a zip for easy pillow-insert removal, and piping to frame the edges. The finished cover will look rather high-end.

SIZE

50cm (19¾in) square

SKILLS USED

- Making piping (page 92)
- Using sew-in interfacing (page 54)
- Straight stitch (page 26)
- Quilting (page 56)
- Sewing a seam (page 24)
- Adding a zip (page 91)
- Top-stitch (page 27)
- Notching and clipping (page 25)
- Finishing seams with zigzag stitch (page 90)
- Adding a tassel (page 93)

PATTERN NOTES

All seam allowances are 5mm (¼in) unless otherwise stated.

YOU WILL NEED

Fabric:

- 114 x 70cm (45 x 27½in) of canvas with a pretty print
- 56 x 45.75cm (22 x 18in) piece (or one Fat Quarter) of coordinating solid fabric, for the piping

Interfacing:

- 114 x 70cm (45 x 27½in) of cotton-polyester mix medium-weight sew-in wadding / batting (such as 279 Cotton Mix 80/20 by Vlieseline®)

Everything else:

- 200cm (78¾in) of 6mm (¼in) thick cotton piping cord
- 48cm (19in) long continuous zip
- Two skeins of stranded embroidery thread / floss, for making the tassel
- 51cm (20in) square pillow insert
- Basic sewing tools (see page 8), including a walking foot, zipper foot and a needle with a large eye

TO CUT

From the canvas fabric:

- 51cm (20in) square, for the front panel
- Two 51 x 28cm (20 x 11in) pieces, for the back panels
- Two 5cm (2in) squares, for the zipper end tabs

From the solid fabric:

- 4cm (1½in) wide bias-cut strips, joined to make a continuous strip measuring 180cm (71in) long

From the interfacing:

- 55cm (21½in) square, to back the front panel
- Two 55 x 31cm (21½ x 12¼in) pieces, to back the back panels

Continuous zip

This is a length of zip that you can purchase as a roll or by the metre (or yard), with just a zip pull and no stopper. This means you can cut it to any length you want. This is great for projects like our pillow cover, where the zip is an unusual length.

However, as there is no stopper, you'll need to make sure the zip ends are secured at some stage, so the zip pull doesn't slide off. Don't worry, we'll cover this in the project.

Instructions

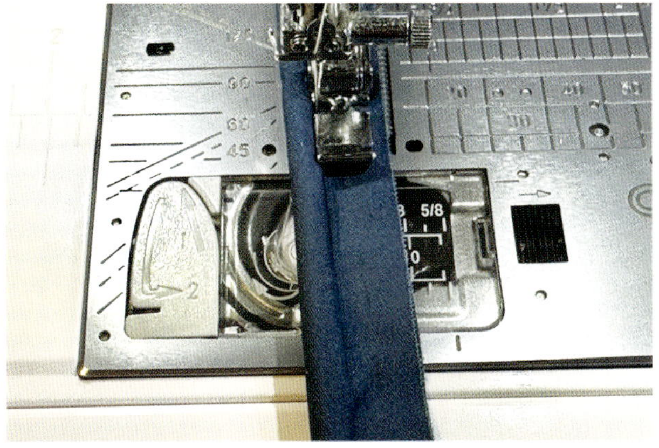

1 Make the piping as detailed on page 92, this time taking care to leave the ends of the piping unstitched, so these can be joined later.

2 Centre the large canvas square over the square of wadding / batting and secure with a few pins. Draw a line diagonally on the canvas square, 3cm (1¼in) from one corner, with a fabric marker. From this line, and at the same distance, draw another line. Attach the walking foot to your sewing machine and attach the guide bar to the machine foot. Sew the first line as shown. Sew the second line and place the guide bar on the first line as shown. Repeat across the whole panel, to the opposite corner, resting the spacer bar on the previous quilt line as you stitch the next line, until the square is covered in diagonal parallel lines.

3 To make the 45-degree cross-hatch grid, repeat Step 2 from a corner adjacent to where you started your first set of quilt lines, and work to the opposite corner.

4 Once the square has been quilted, trim the wadding / batting back to the size of the canvas square. Repeat Steps 2–4 for the canvas back panels.

5 Turn under one edge of each 5cm (2in) square by 5mm (¼in).

6 With the folded edges pointing towards the zip teeth, lightly glue the squares to each end of the zip, their RS facing up – you will need to pull the zip slightly open to move the slider out of the way. Leave to dry completely.

7 Once dry, trim the squares to the width of the zip; these are your zip tabs.

8 Centre the zip along one long edge of a back panel, RS together and with the right-hand edge of the zip matching the edge of the back panel. Attach the zipper foot on the sewing machine, then sew along the edge. Fold the zip away from the panel, so its RS is facing up, then top-stitch along the edge of the back panel where the zip is attached. Repeat on the other side of the zip with the remaining panels. One your zip is 'sandwiched' between the two panels, trim back the zip tabs so they're flush with the back panels.

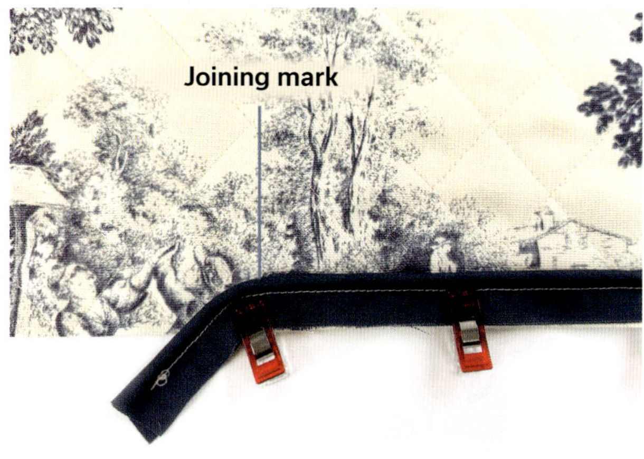

9 Make a mark at the centre bottom of the front panel – this indicates where the two ends of your piping will meet later. Lay the piping along the edge of the front panel, the starting end of the piping staggering the centre mark by 2.5cm (1in) – see the blue 'joining mark' line in the image above. Note that the raw edge of the piping fabric should be facing out and flush with the raw edge of the panel. Pin or clip the piping in place.

10 Pin or clip the rest of the piping in place on the front panel. At the corners, clip into the tape to help the piping curve, taking care not to cut into the piping stitching.

11 Using the zipper foot, and beginning from the joining mark, sew the piping on to the front panel, stitching as close to the piping cord as you possibly can.

12 When you get close to where the piping start and finishing ends meet, stop sewing. Over the joining mark, cross the two ends of the piping over each other, allowing the finishing end to overhang by about 2.5cm (1in). Both piping ends should bend away from the work. Clip in place, then stitch across the crossover to secure, as shown. Trim the overhang excess so it's level with the raw edge of the pillow cover.

13 Open the zipper about halfway then pin or clip the front and back panels RS together. Opening the zip is really important; if you forget to do it, you will lock yourself out and the unpicker will be needed!

14 Sew all around the edge of the cover, stitching close to the piping cord as you go.

15 Snip across the corners to reduce bulk.

16 Finish the raw edges with a zigzag stitch.

17 Turn the pillow cover the right way out and attach the tassel to the zipper pull. To finish, stuff the pillow insert inside the cover then zip the cover closed.

Techniques

USING CANVAS

Canvas is a gorgeous fabric to work with – mostly. Let's go over the good points first.

Most sewing machines love to sew canvas because it is thick, so it feeds through the machine really well. The wealth of colour and pattern available is mind blowing (and it seems to be expanding each year), and you can find canvas in several widths and weaves too, to tailor to your project perfectly.

And now for the bad news. Canvas frays. A lot. And the more you handle it, the more it comes apart. As a general rule, the looser the weave, the more it will fray, so you'll need to work with it carefully.

There are a few things that can be done to minimize fraying in woven fabrics like canvas. The first: consider ironing a thin fusible interfacing on the wrong side of the canvas to hold it all together (**A**). I love using medium-weight fusible cotton interlining (such as G740 by Vlieseline®) for this job because it adds almost no weight to the fabric but stabilizes it wonderfully.

The second is to consider pinking the edges (**B**). If you're not familiar with pinking, this is simply cutting the edges of fabric with special scissors that have a scalloped or zigzagged edge. Pinking won't stop the fray but it will slow it down. If you decide to use pinking shears, be careful not to cut too deeply into the edge; it can eat into your seam allowance.

A

B

MAKING LINED SLIP POCKETS

There are a few different sorts of pockets that we can put into a bag, and one of the simplest is a wide, lined slip pocket. A slip pocket is simply a piece of fabric that is secured to your main fabric on the bottom and sides only, with the top left open – you'll have seen them inside bags, on shirt breast pockets and skirts. My approach to slip pockets gives you a more robust pocket: I like to line them as they wear better. In addition, a lined pocket means you don't have to worry about sewing the edges or making them neat; all of the raw edges are hidden inside the pocket. And did I mention making a lined slip pocket is easy?

1 Interface the outer pocket panel with light-weight fusible interfacing (I'm using iron-on, medium-weight interlining). Don't worry about interfacing the lining.

2 Place the lining panel and outer pocket panel right sides together, matching the edges. Pin or clip in place.

3 Sew a seam along the longest edges only, leaving the shorter sides open.

4 Turn the pocket out through one of the open sides. Then, press so that the top and bottom seams are perfect, as shown.

5 Decide which is the top edge (a directional print will help you make this decision; otherwise, you choose!). Top-stitch twice along the top edge: the first time very narrowly, approx. 2mm (1/8in) from the folded edge; then the second time 5mm (1/4in) down from the folded edge.

ATTACHING LINED SLIP POCKETS

The pattern will tell you where to sew your pocket to the main project, and the distance from certain edges too.

1 Position the pocket on the right side of the appropriate fabric panel as instructed in the pattern, making sure the pocket outer is facing up and the lining side is facing the project. Ensure the project is dead straight too. Pin in place.

Centring pockets

We will be centring our slip pocket in the upcoming tote bag, and you'll be pleased to learn this is simple to do. Just fold your pocket in half vertically, finger-press to make a crease then open it out. You can either do the same on the panel of your project you're attaching it to, or measure and mark the centre with a ruler. After both centres have been found, you can line up the centre marks on both pieces, then pin the pocket in place before sewing.

2 Edge-stitch along the bottom of the pocket (this is to echo the row of stitching along the top edge of the pocket).

3 Tack / baste the sides of the pockets in place with a 3mm (⅛in) seam allowance – don't worry that these are raw edges, as they'll be hidden in a seam later.

4 Slip pockets can sag when they're over a particular width. This is an opportunity to divide them into smaller compartments, achieved by sewing vertical lines through all fabric layers. Dividing is easy – decide what you want to put in the pockets (mobile / cellphone, pen etc.), measure their width plus a little extra for ease, mark the fabric, then stitch accordingly.

BOXING CORNERS

A flat bag can be quite useful for laptops and books; but for anything thicker and with a little more volume, you'll need to introduce a base to your bag. There are various methods, but the quickest way is to box the corners. This involves cutting squares from the corners of your joined fabric pieces, then sewing them in such a way as to turn the bottom into a base.

To account for the 'loss' in width and height, extra measurements are added to the fabric dimensions – these measurements have to be carefully calculated so that the boxed corners don't upset the placement of pockets and handles, and so on. Don't worry, most sewing patterns will do this calculation for you.

Boxing the corners is the same process for both the outer and the lining of a bag.

1 On the two bottom corners of your bag draw an exact square, using the measurements directed in the pattern.

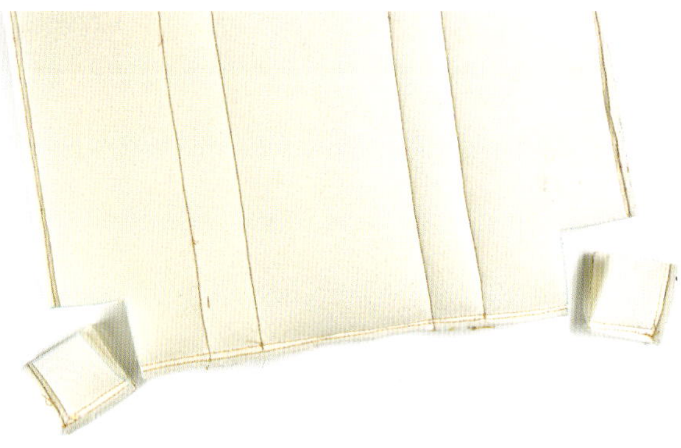

2 Now the (slightly) scary bit: cut out the marked squares at both corners.

3 At one corner, pinch the bottom seam and side seam RS together, making sure the bottom seams match and are centred. Pin or clip in place. Repeat at the other corner.

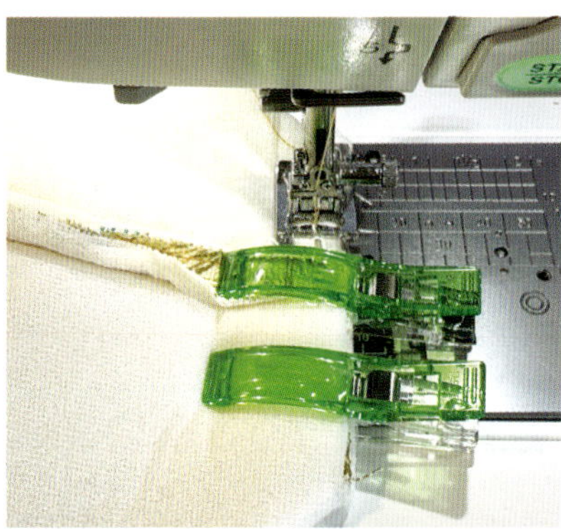

4 Sew right across one pinned or clipped corner, reverse stitching at the beginning and end of the seam for extra strength. Repeat for the other corner.

5 Turn the bag outer RS out. Very gently persuade the corners out so that they are as sharp as possible, using the eraser end of a pencil.

Simple Mini Tote Bag

Everyone needs a tote bag in their lives! I am quite ready to stand by that decree. Tote bags are so useful, especially when they have boxed corners like this one as they can hold a surprisingly large amount of stuff. The slightly wider straps on this tote make it comfortable to carry too, while the minimalist design is great to show off a lovely print.

SIZE

Approx. 27cm (10¾in) wide x 11cm (4¼in) deep x 27cm (10¾in) tall, not including handles; 43cm (17in) tall including handles

SKILLS USED

- Using canvas (page 102)
- Using fusible interfacing (page 34)
- Straight stitch (page 26)
- Sewing a seam (page 24)
- Turning through (page 35)
- Top-stitching (page 27)
- Using foam interfacing (page 81)
- Edge-stitching (page 27)
- Boxing corners (page 105)
- Making lined slip pockets (page 103)
- Attaching lined slip pockets (page 104)

PATTERN NOTES

All seam allowances are 5mm (¼in) unless otherwise stated.

YOU WILL NEED

Fabric:

- 114 x 50cm (45 x 19¾in) of Fabric 1 (canvas), for the bag outer
- 114 x 50cm (45 x 19¾in) of Fabric 2 (cotton), for the bag lining and outer pocket lining
- 114 x 50cm (45 x 19¾in) of Fabric 3 (coordinating cotton), for the internal pockets
- 60cm (23¾in) length of 2.5cm (1in) wide light-weight leather, vegan leather or cork, for the handle trims

Interfacing:

- 90 x 100cm (35½ x 39½in) of medium-weight fusible cotton interlining (such as G740 by Vlieseline®)
- 72 x 100cm (28½ x 39½in) of light-weight sew-in foam interfacing (such as Style-Vil by Vlieseline®)

Everything else:

- 225cm (88½in) of 4cm (1½in) wide cotton webbing, for the bag handles
- Double-sided tape
- Basic sewing tools (see page 8), including a walking foot for sewing the leather (or cork) strip

TO CUT

From Fabric 1 (canvas):

- Two 39.5 x 33cm (15½ x 13in) pieces for the front and back outer bag panels
- One 15cm (6in) square for the outer pocket panel on the bag front outer

From Fabric 2 (cotton):

- Two 38 x 32cm (15 x 12½in) pieces for the front and back lining bag panels
- One 15cm (6in) square for the lining pocket panel on the bag front outer

From Fabric 3 (coordinating cotton):

- Four 38 x 14cm (15 x 5½in) pieces for the pocket panels for the internal bag pockets

From the handle trim material:

- Two 30cm (12in) lengths of 2.5cm (1in) wide lightweight leather, faux leather or cork

From the medium-weight fusible cotton interlining:

- Two 39.5 x 33cm (15½ x 13in) pieces for interfacing the front and back outer bag panel
- One 15cm (6in) square for interfacing the outer pocket panel on the bag front outer
- Two 38 x 14cm (15 x 5½in) pieces for interfacing the outer pocket panels for the internal bag pockets

From the light-weight sew-in foam interfacing:

- Two 43 x 36cm (17 x 14¼in) for interfacing the front and back outer bag panel

From the webbing:

- Two 107cm (42¼in) long pieces, for the handles

Instructions

1 Make up the handles first: round the ends of the handle trims, using a mug or something similar as a template to draw and cut around.

2 Centre then stick the trims to the webbing straps with double-sided tape, then top-stitch into place.

3 Fuse the medium-weight cotton interlining to the WS of the front and back outer bag panels and the outer pocket panel on the bag front outer.

4 Pin the interfaced outer pocket panel for the bag front outer to the lining pocket panel for the bag front outer, RS together.

5 Sew the top and bottom seams only, then turn the pocket RS out through one of the open sides. Press so that the seam sits neatly along the edge.

6 Top-stitch the top edge of the pocket twice as described in Step 5 on page 103.

7 Find the centres of the outer bag front and the outer pocket panel. Measure 7cm (2¾in) down from the top edge of the outer front panel then mark and pin the top edge of the pocket onto the mark, matching the centres. Top-stitch just the bottom edge of the pocket in place; for the sides, machine tack / baste in place with a 3mm (⅛in) SA.

Why tack / baste the sides?

Like a regular slip pocket, we are tacking / basting the sides of the pocket to temporarily secure them in place. The raw edges will be hidden (and secured) later, when we sew the bag straps to the bag.

8 Centre the interfaced outer front and back bag panels onto a piece of foam interfacing, pin then machine tack / baste all around the perimeter with a mm (⅛in) SA. Trim the foam back to the size of the outer bag panels.

9 From each side edge of the interfaced outer front and back panels, measure in by 10cm (4in); indicate a vertical line on the bag panel with a couple of markings with a fabric pen.

10 Stick a length of double-sided tape at each end of one webbing piece, then position the webbing over the outer front bag panel – the raw ends of the webbing should be flush with the bottom edge of the bag panel, the long edges should sit inside the markings from Step 9, and the 'loop' of the webbing should overhang at the top of the bag. You should notice that the webbing straddles the raw edges of the pocket and covers them.

11 Edge-stitch the handle in place: start from one long edge on one webbing end, sew up by 28cm (11in), sew across the width of the webbing then sew down to the bottom edge again. Repeat with the other webbing end (see the white stitching in the photograph above). You will be sewing through all layers, and you may find that using your walking foot for this step will help if your sewing machine is struggling. Attach the handle in the same way for the outer back bag panel, repeating Steps 10 and 11.

12 Pin or clip the two outer bag panels RS together, lining up the bottom ends of the handles. Sew the sides and bottom only, leaving the top edge open – you will need a walking foot for this step! Leave the outer bag inside out.

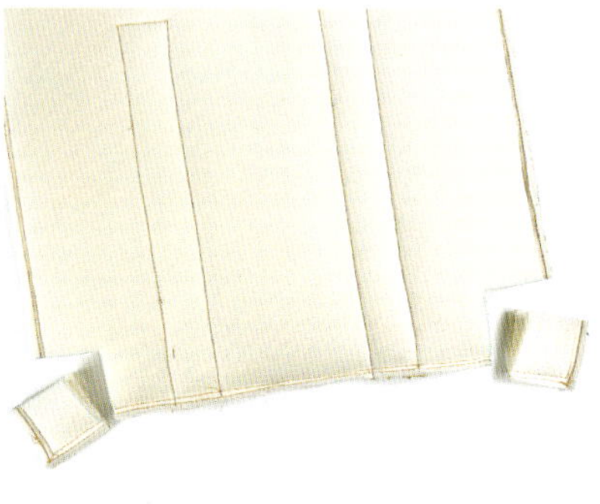

13 Mark and cut out a 5cm (2in) square at the bottom two corners of the outer bag. Box the corners as outlined on page 105. Turn the outer bag RS out then set aside.

14 Interface the WS of the outer pieces for the internal bag pockets. Make the lined slip pockets as per Steps 4–6 on pages 109 and 110.

15 Find and mark the centre of the bag lining panels and the internal bag pockets – I folded my pieces in half vertically then opened them out, creating a crease on each piece. Measure 9cm (3½in) down from the top edge of the lining and add a few marks horizontally with a fabric marker.

16 With the internal pockets the right way out (the side with the interfacing behind it should be facing up), line up the top of the pockets with the marks made in Step 15, making sure the centre markings or creases match. Pin then sew the pockets in place as described on page 104.

17 To stop the pocket sagging, and to create smaller, useful compartments, divide them up with some vertical lines of stitching – ensure you reverse stitch at the beginning and end of each stitch line for extra strength.

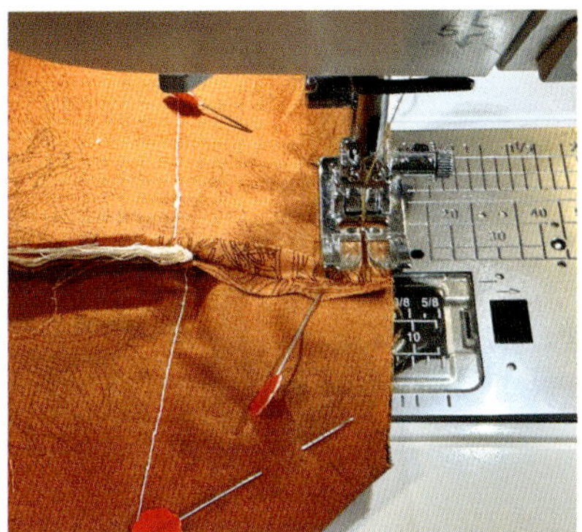

18 Now to sew together the bag lining. With RS together and the internal bag pockets perfectly matched, sew the sides and base of the lining as for the bag outer, this time leaving a 10cm (4in) turning gap in the bottom seam of the lining. Box the bottom corners of the lining exactly the same as you did for the outer bag.

19 With the outer bag RS out and the bag lining WS out, pull the lining over the outer bag. Adjust the bag lining so its seams match those for the outer bag. The RS of both bags should be facing each other, the top edges of both bags should align, and the handles will be pointing down and between the two layers.

20 Sew all around the top edge of the bag leaving no gaps.

21 Turn the bag out through the gap in the lining, as shown. Pull the lining out of the outer bag then sew the gap closed by machine – this will be stronger than hand stitches.

22 Stuff the lining down into the bag and press the top edge so that it is perfect. On the RS of the outer bag, top-stitch two rows of stitching all around – one 3mm (⅛in) from the top edge, then one 5mm (¼in) from the top edge.

Moving on

Congratulations for reaching this stage! If you have been working your way through this book, you will have reached that happy point where you can go out into the world and look for new sewing projects to beautify your life. The skills that you have learned are all very transferable and this opens the whole world of sewing creativity. Have a look at some of these examples and you will see what I mean.

Pot Holder

A pot holder is a wonderful pattern to have handy if you need a quick make, a last-minute gift, or want to sew something with a piece of beloved fabric. I actually printed this fabric (which is a canvas fabric) myself using some paper craft stamps and fabric-friendly ink pads. The ink is not only washable, but the stamping means there will never be another pot holder quite like it.

To make the pot holder, first cut a square of fabric that's about 5cm (2in) larger than your hand all around. Based on this square, cut a rectangle from the same fabric that is the same width but a third taller. Lay each fabric piece over a slightly larger piece of sew-in wadding / batting, then place these over an even larger backing piece – the right side of the backing should be facing down, and the right side of the fabric pieces should be facing up. Pin the layers in place – see page 54 for more details. Quilt all over each quilt sandwich with 45-degree cross-hatched lines. After quilting, trim the layers back to the size of the main fabric pieces, as in Step 3 on page 65. Round two corners of the square quilt sandwich, and all corners of the rectangle quilt sandwich, as per Step 4 on page 66.

Make up a long length of bias binding as described on page 59. Attach it to the edge of the square quilt sandwich without the rounded corners, as detailed in Step 3 on page 60, the binding running edge to edge. Lay the square quilt sandwich over the rectangle quilt sandwich, matching the round corners. Sewing within the seam allowance, sew the square quilt sandwich to the rectangle quilt sandwich, stitching around the sides and rounded bottom edge only. Attach the remaining length of bias binding all around, following the instructions on pages 60 and 61. To finish, add a leather loop tab for hanging the pot holder as described on page 36 – just make the leather strip longer.

Card Wallet

This is one of my favourite tiny makes, and is perfect for using every scrap of fabric in the most beautiful way possible. These are fantastically useful in a handbag for cards (as intended) but also for other small items that you don't want to go migrating around the bottom of your bag on their own – my friend keeps a couple of her favourite tea bags in hers, because you never know!

The wallet and its template are made in virtually the same way as the Felt Laptop Sleeve on page 72; the only differences are it's on a smaller scale, and the lining and outers are sewn right sides together then bagged out like the table mat (see Steps 3, 4, 6 and 7 on pages 40 and 41).

The fastening is a plastic snap fastener this time, placed on the flap instead of on a strap. You'll need a special pair of pliers to fit these fastenings; sometimes the fitting tool comes with the pack of fastenings, so it's worth investing in such a set if you're buying them for the first time.

Hexie Pillow

You may be familiar with the English Paper Piecing technique, where you cut out shapes like diamonds or hexagons from paper, wrap fabric around each paper shape, then sew the shapes together? Well, this pillow uses a variation on that technique. Rather than sewing the hexagon ('hexie') shaped pieces together to make your project, in this modern update the hexies are simply quilted onto a background panel, without being joined together initially.

The pillow is made in a similar way to the one on page 94; the only differences are the hexies are adhered in place (either with iron-on, paper-backed adhesive web or fabric glue) before the front panel is quilted, the straight-line quilting mimics the angles of the hexies, and there's no piping. It is quick, easy and, best of all, you have most of the techniques under your belt already!

Place Mat

I love mats for my house. They are handy and there is always a use for them. It's astounding how much they cheer up a room and, rather like throw pillows, you can never have too many! Re-jig this design for the festive period by choosing some seasonal fabrics, and dress your table with candles and fir branches for instant folk chic!

To make the mat, cut four 15cm (6in) squares – two from one fabric, and two from another. Sew contrasting squares right sides together in pairs along one edge, open out then press the seam allowances towards the darker fabric. Sew the two pairs right sides together, matching the seams in the middle, to make a grid of four squares. Press the seam allowances open.

Use this patchwork panel as a template to cut out a square of backing fabric and a square of wadding / batting. Make a quilt sandwich with the three layers: backing fabric on the bottom (face down), wadding / batting in the middle, and the patchwork panel on top (face up) – see page 54 for reminder. Pin then quilt the place mat as desired – I used a wave pattern (see pages 56 and 57). Lay a dinner plate over the quilted layers, use it to draw a circle then cut out your circle shape from the layers.

Make up a long length of binding in the same or coordinating fabric, as per page 59, then attach it all around the edge of the mat as detailed on pages 60 and 61 to finish.

Templates

GOLDFISH TEMPLATES & POSITIONING DIAGRAM

Appliqué Storage Cube (page 84)
Cut 4 of each body part

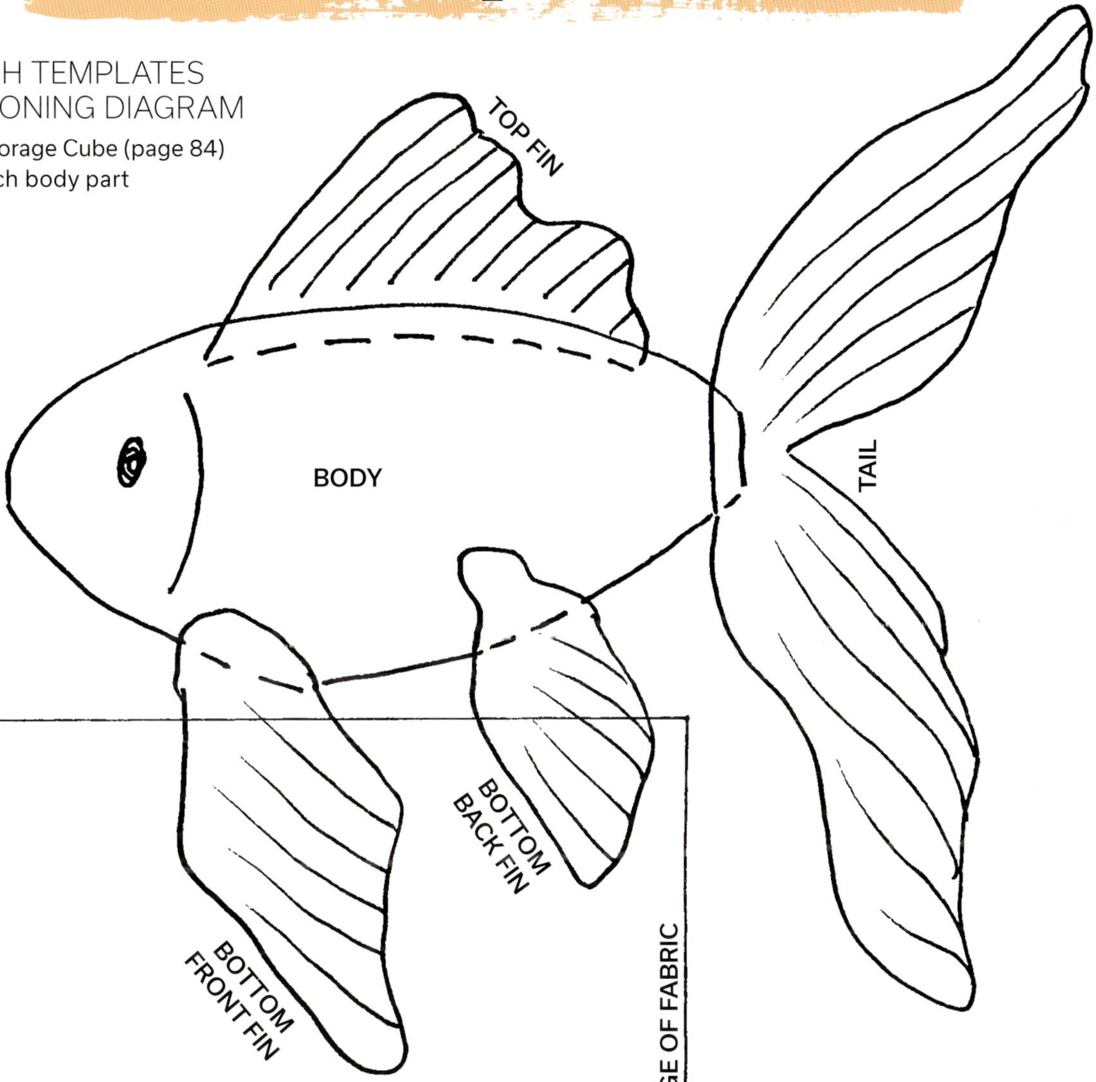

TOP FIN
BODY
TAIL
BOTTOM BACK FIN
BOTTOM FRONT FIN

DART TEMPLATE

Easy Trinket Tray (page 44)
Use the cut-out corner of the template to cut out a triangular dart from the fabric

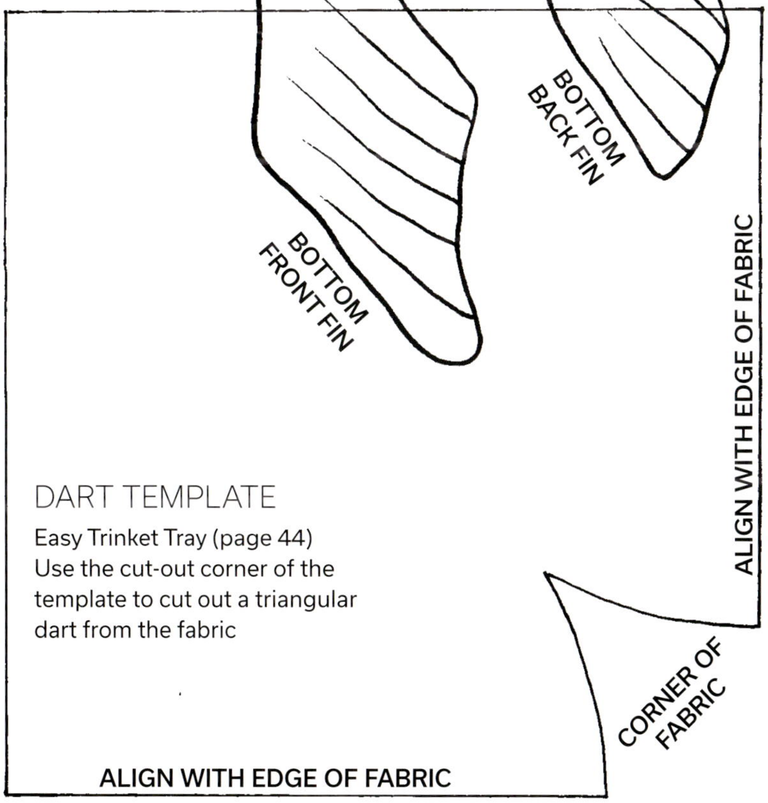

ALIGN WITH EDGE OF FABRIC
CORNER OF FABRIC
ALIGN WITH EDGE OF FABRIC

Index